LURES FOR GAME,
COARSE AND SEA FISHING

To Tom Saville
with thanks
for your kind help.

Never mind

To Perry Adams,
As Tom did not have
another in stock the
tight bugger he sent
you this one.
Best wishes
Jr. [signature]

Lures for Game, Coarse and Sea Fishing

S. D. (TAFF) PRICE

DRAWINGS BY ROBIN ARMSTRONG

ADAM & CHARLES BLACK
LONDON

FIRST PUBLISHED 1972
BY ADAM AND CHARLES BLACK LIMITED
4, 5 AND 6 SOHO SQUARE LONDON WIV 6AD

© 1972 S. D. (TAFF) PRICE

ISBN 0 7136 1305 X

Printed in Great Britain by
C. Tinling & Co. Ltd, London and Prescot

Contents

Illustrations

BLACK AND WHITE

COLOUR

Preface

Since the Second World War, and to the greatest extent during the 1960–1970 decade, the interest and participation in fly-fishing has increased at a greater pace than ever before. This upsurge applies to other forms of fishing as well, but it was for the fly fisherman and fly tyer that this book was written.

The biggest single factor which contributed to the big increase in the numbers of fly fishermen, was the construction of numerous reservoirs in Great Britain, particularly around the industrial areas where the demand for water was greatest. As the stocking of these waters with trout became a standard policy, amongst other facilities made available to the public for recreational purposes, vast areas of attractive trout fishing water became available at a reasonable price to a degree, never before seen in Britain. Pollution had reduced many fine trout rivers to open sewers, and as the amount of angling of this sort grew less, that which remained automatically became more expensive and exclusive.

The proximity of the new waters to the industrial areas previously mentioned, was another vital factor in the growth of the interest in fly-fishing, for these areas contained rapidly enlarging populations mostly confined to mainly urban districts.

This mode of living had the natural psychological reaction in that a desire to escape from the confinement was created, and an urge to return to the more simple pursuits and out-door pleasures which are deep-rooted in modern man's subsconscious. Add to this the increase in the prosperity of the general public, and the growth of the means of easy transport (the motor car), and the whole picture of the reason for the interest growth in fly-fishing rapidly unfolds.

I have no wish to enlarge further on this aspect of our environmental transitions, interesting as the theme may be, and the foregoing paragraphs are merely an introduction or explanation as to how the idea for this book was conceived.

Because of the circumstances I have described, it was only natural that this vast influx of new blood into angling would produce a new brand of angler, and bring a new approach to an old established sport. Amongst these was Derek Price, now known only as 'Taff', by all who know him well.

He was born in 1934 at Barmouth in North Wales, educated at Barmouth County Grammar School, which he left to become a Scientific Assistant at Woolwich Arsenal. He is now a sales representative for a packaging company, and it is my personal opinion that he settled for this career as it enabled him to travel and also indulge in his main two loves, fishing and fly-tying. His fishing interests include both Game and Sea angling, and I referred to his main two loves because his others are Natural History, Folk Music, Writing poetry, and reading. Such erudition applied to an interest such as angling was bound to be productive, and this book is the result.

Taff is an individualist, preferring to fish alone rather than be a member of any club, syndicate or association, and this is reflected in his fly-tying. Although inumerable books have been produced on flies and fly-tying, an enquiring mind can always perceive improvements or variations, and as Taff comes definitely within this category, gradually he began to evolve variations of standard patterns, and then patterns of original design.

A further development was the channelling of his main interest into that of lures and lure fishing, not only because this method was becoming increasingly popular on the reservoirs, but also because he saw their potential in other angling spheres such as Salmon, Sea Trout and saltwater fishing.

Once again I must add that this subject had been dealt with several times in the past by other authors, but they were in the main our American cousins, whose native game fish and fishing

waters lent themselves to the development of this type of artificial
fly. I had done some of this work myself in the past, and was very
happy to see that it was bearing fruit, the increasing use of the lure
in reservoirs being obvious proof of this. However, I had merely
touched on the subject in volumes devoted in the main to other
types of flies, so I was doubly pleased to see the growth of Taff's
book, and extremely happy to go over his final Manuscript and
pass it on to Mr. Archie Black my publisher.

In his search for established patterns in the sphere of lure making,
and fishing, Taff made use of the services of many famous (and not
so well known) individuals and fly tying companies, and gives
ample credit to those who helped him. He has produced his book
to show the lure in its modern form, based on his own experience,
the experience of other present day anglers, plus the best ideas of
the past, and although it is aimed primarily at the British Angler,
just as I thought that 'foreign' flies could be useful to us here,
I am sure that any of our brother anglers overseas who care to
take it up will find a wealth of information useful to them as well.

I am looking forward to the final publishing date so that I can
put this book amongst the other worthwhile volumes in my
library.

John Veniard

Introduction

In the past, most books that concerned themselves with the art of fly dressing, and in particular those books that listed patterns, treated lures and the like as 'Cinderella' flies. Affording them little mention and only giving a few examples.

At the present time in this country, the lure/fly is becoming a more important weapon in the flyfisherman's repertoire. The reason for this of course is due to the increase in fishing waters throughout the country, holding larger fish and allowing a greater number of anglers to participate in the fine sport of fly fishing.

The dressings to be found in this book are the work of many professional and amateur fly dressers, the bulk coming from British sources. The book also includes many International patterns, these are included for comparison, for their availability from commercial sources, where there is no British counterpart, and also for their fame and popularity.

Amongst the lures and flies listed in this book are Streamers, Bucktails, Hairwing Salmon Flies, Surface Lures, and lures for Coarse and Sea Fish. Something, I hope, for everyone.

I am indebted to all those who helped me compile this book, giving encouragement, advice and providing the patterns that grace the following pages. It goes without saying without them there would have been no book.

All materials used for the dressing of lures mentioned in this book, are readily available in this country.

Those of us who dress flies know only too well of the service rendered by the firm of E. Veniard Ltd, Thornton Heath, Surrey. They are world renowned for their postal service of materials and fly dressing tools. The results of our labours would be a drab and sorry collection of flies indeed if it were not for the colourful and exotic feathers gleaned from all corners of the world by this firm.

In recent years fly fishing and of course fly dressing has become a growth interest, not for a privileged few but for a greater strata of the population. This explosion of interest has resulted in much experimentation and many types of fly and lure have been developed.

Veniards have kept pace with this growth and from their Surrey warehouses fly dressers are assured of receiving the traditional and modern materials necessary to pursue their hobby or profession. My thanks go to the Directors and staff of this company for their advice and help in selecting materials for many of the flies and lures that appear in this book.

Taff Price

Footscray, 1971

[1]

Streamer and Bucktail Flies and Lures

Streamer and bucktail flies, in the main, are lures tied to represent the various forms of bait fish, and the fry of some of the larger species. There are however some exceptions: a number of lures are tied to represent other forms of aquatic life and in some cases terrestrial creatures can be imitated by this form of lure. All these creatures, especially the small fish, form an important part of the diet of predatory fish, not at specific times during the year, but throughout the fishing season and more so than many anglers think.

Streamer flies differ from bucktail lures in the winging medium. The streamer relies on feathers, and the bucktail, as its name suggests, utilises the hair of various animals. The original lures were no doubt tied with the deer's tail hence the appellation 'Bucktail'.

In the United States this kind of lure or fly has been used to a far greater extent than in Great Britain, and though much of the pioneering work and invention of new patterns is the result of American inventiveness, we in this country have been using this kind of fly in one form or another for quite some considerable time. The multi-hook lure beloved by some seatrout anglers is an example of this.

Many of the well known lake and seatrout flies of Great Britain were adapted by the Americans and 'Streamerised' as it were, by use of the long shank hook in order to give the fly a longer fishlike appearance. The Alexandra and Coachman flies are two that come readily to mind. So it is not inconceivable that an American sportsman could at this moment be fishing for 'lunker' Rainbows with elongated standard British patterns, a Bloody Butcher Streamer for example.

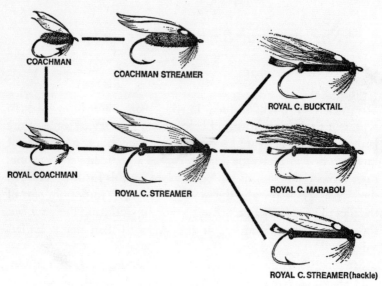

Fig. 1   Evolution of the Streamer and Bucktail

Who of us has not caught the ubiquitous mackerel from the salty sea with the feathered lure? And what after all is the mackerel lure but a streamer fly, albeit a primitive one.

Throughout the world where man relies on fish as part of his staple diet, he has evolved lures of this nature to catch fish. The Eskimo in Alaska for instance is known to have used lures of Polar Bear fur, and it is not unknown for some of the primitive tribes of the Amazon to utilise flowers as a streamer fly to catch some of the many exotic fish that dwell in that Eden of rivers.

I think it reasonably safe to assume that streamer and bucktail flies are as old as man himself, having a lineage longer than some of the more conventional patterns with a history that appears to start with that old nun, Juliana Berners.

A Selection of Lures

The greater availability of trout waters, in the form of reservoirs, has led in recent years to an upsurge of interest and also experimentation in the types of lures that are fished on them. Streamer and bucktail flies figure highly on the list of fish catching flies used by a new breed of angler that does not pay lip service to ancient and hidebound fishing dogma.

Many anglers have adapted the patterns evolved on our new reservoirs to their own rivers and lakes and have accordingly experienced considerable success with them for brown and rainbow trout, seatrout, pike and perch, some of the minnow type creations at times being particularly effective for chub, and what is more both roach and rudd have fallen victim to these same flies. The Atlantic salmon too is not immune to the allure of the streamer and bucktail. Many a fisherman, when all other lures have failed, has resorted to the streamer fly, more in desperation than anything else, and has taken his fish, forever swearing that in certain conditions, there is nothing to beat a Grey Ghost or a Muddler Minnow as the case may be.

Though streamers are becoming more popular, a great number of anglers fight shy of using them. Pike anglers seem content to fish for their quarry with live and dead baits, plugs and spinners and give the streamer fly a miss. Why? Your guess is as good as mine. Good pike can be taken on feather and fur.

Types of Streamer Flies

This kind of fly can basically be divided into two groups:
1. The direct representation or an impression of a natural fish, etc.
2. The flasher or attractor patterns.

As with conventional flies, a trout will take a streamer or a bucktail because it prompts a response; triggers off a reaction in the fishes mind which could be a different one depending on the fly used and the prevailing conditions.

A trout will take a streamer of the representative type, because it is hungry. It recognises in the fly food that it has eaten before. It will also take from anger, often savagely striking at what it con-

B

siders to be a rival for food, when the streamer or bucktail moves into the trout's own private preserve. The 'anger' take can also occur because of the bizarre and foreign appearance of the streamer; the rejection of the unusual. This has its counterpart in the bird world. When a bright coloured cage bird escapes it is often attacked by the wild species of the garden.

I think too that the trout take from sheer devilment, in a crazy *joie de vivre*. This unusual lack of caution has caused the downfall of many a fish that for years had eluded the skill and guile of the angler, only to end up on the plate due to that sudden rash, playful mood that had lingered in its tiny brain since it was a fingerling.

Many anglers are under the misapprehension that streamers are only used effectively early in the season or when the waters are cloudy with flood water. This is not so. Streamers can be used successfully in water that is both low and crystal clear and often take fish in these conditions when the smallest nymph and the most cunningly presented dry fly both fail.

Why this is, is to know the mind of the fish and there are few of us yet to have analysed the actions and brain of our trout adversary. If we could psycho-analyse the trout much of the enjoyment of fishing would be lost. Is not the heavier than usual fish—taken when we least expect it—the most remembered? Of course it is. It is the very essence of angling. No matter how much we 'fish think' the imponderable always occurs, and thank God for it. That heavier than normal fish that takes us by surprise and is caught when all reason dictates that we haven't a snowball's chance in hell of catching it is the joy of angling.

It is true to say that in this country the streamer fly is used in the main on our stillwater reservoirs, so most commercially tied flies are constructed with these waters in mind. For stillwater, the winging of our lures must lie close to the hook shank, and the attraction of such flies rests with the angler and how he works his fly and the way he retrieves and manipulates his line. When fishing fast water, some consideration must be given to the dressing of the fly, for in fast water a normal stillwater fly's wing is forced down, masking the flash of the body, and offering the trout no more than a mis-shapen bundle of feathers that will prove as attractive to the trout as a shuttlecock. So when tying flies for fast moving rivers the wing of our fly must be raised approximately 30 to 45 degrees to combat this distortion of the fly in the swift currents.

Streamer and Bucktail construction

As for conventional fishing flies the materials involved in the construction of our streamers and bucktails are wide and various and to the traditional media is added each year new materials due to the ingenuity of the modern fly dresser.

BODIES

Gold and silver flat tinsels, embossed tinsels, floss silks left untouched or sometimes coated in clear varnish for durability, seals fur, polar bear fur, coloured wools, mohair, chenille etc.

STREAMER WINGING

The saddle hackles of both game and domestic cocks, and dyed in various colours. The dyed hackles of the badger variety make a very good winging medium, the black list providing the natural lateral line that occurs in many fish.

Cree or Plymouth Rock hackles with their barred effect imitate the natural markings on such fish as the perch, and the mottling of the loach and bullhead species. Other patterns utilise the green and bronze herls of the resplendent peacock. The herl of the ostrich too is used in a large selection of flies. Some patterns call for whole feather wings, strips of swan or goose feathers natural and dyed are used on their own or as a combination multicoloured built wing of two or three colours. The Mickey Finn, and Parmachene Belle are just two examples that come to mind. A feather that I am particularly fond of is the Marabou. It is an extremely mobile feather which fish find irresistible, black being particularly effective, though other colours are used in a variety of fish catching patterns. In New Zealand, the split feathers of various game birds are used to make flies of the Matuka, and whole feather wing styles. Some streamer patterns incorporate fur as well as feathers in their construction, the bucktail giving extra body to the wing.

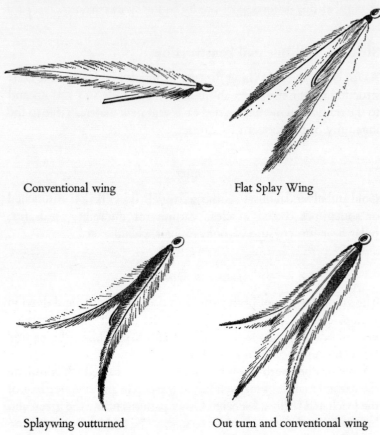

Conventional wing   Flat Splay Wing

Splaywing outturned   Out turn and conventional wing

Fig. 2   Streamer Winging

BUCKTAIL WINGING

Here again a wealth of different furs, usually from the tails of mammals, is used for the wing of the bucktail fly. One of the most common is bucktail itself, both natural and dyed in the multitude of colours that modern dyes provide. The tails of the various squirrels of the world are also used to a great degree. In this country of course the common grey squirrel is used. The long guard fur of the brown, black and polar bears, the fur of 'Brock' the badger, and the long fur of a variety of monkeys can be utilised.

The little stoat, provides the wing of some patterns, the well-known Stoat fly is an example of this. To these furs one can add a legion of other furs both natural and man made, amongst them

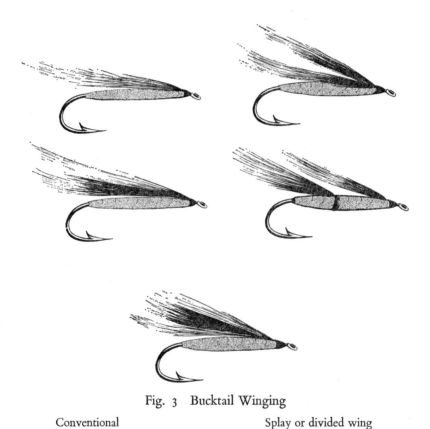

Fig. 3   Bucktail Winging

Conventional   Splay or divided wing
Bi-coloured   Double wing
                        Tri-coloured

such exotic materials as Impala tail, moose mane, opossum, skunk, bison, and ringcat, in fact the fur of any animal that has a long fur mane, tail or pelt.

HACKLES

Hackles on streamer flies are there to provide simulated gills, the underbody of a fish, or there just to provide mobility. Many patterns have no hackle whatsoever. The types are shown in Fig. 4:

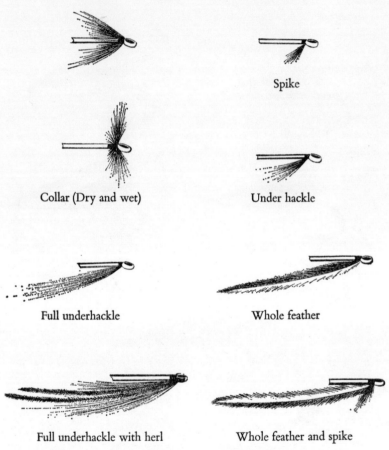

Spike

Collar (Dry and wet)   Under hackle

Full underhackle   Whole feather

Full underhackle with herl   Whole feather and spike

Fig. 4   Hackles or Underbodies

the collar type hackle; the spike or throat hackle; the full hackle extending to the barb of the hook; a full whole feather under-body; and finally, an under-body and spike hackle combined.

The wording hackle of course is a traditional appellation, a far better description in most cases would be under-body.

CHEEKS AND SHOULDERS

The universal feather for the cheeks of the majority of patterns is the attractive jungle cock neck feather. Alas this beautiful bird is now becoming rare in the world, and a ban on the import of feathers and capes is now imposed. The days when we can use this beautiful feather are therefore numbered, and the capes etc. only available whilst present stocks last. A further mention of the Jungle cock is made in the brief chapter on fly dressing tips. There are a number of other media we can use instead of the natural jungle cock feather. Messrs. Veniards of Thornton Heath purvey an imitation plastic jungle cock which is not a bad copy of the natural feather. Quite a few patterns for both freshwater and sea fishing now incorporate the non-tarnish Mylar strip, providing that flash and glitter so necessary in streamer lures. As far as shoulders are concerned, Golden Pheasant tippet, Lady Amhurst tippets, the body feathers of most wild fowl such as Widgeon, Teal, Mallard, Summerduck are used in some patterns, whilst body feathers from the Partridge, Grouse and other game birds are utilised in others.

THE HEAD AND TAIL

All that remains of our streamer and bucktail fly is the head and tail. Though a small head is required in many flies, some streamer lures often have an exaggerated head, after all it would be a strange fish indeed that had a small pinhead out of all proportion to the rest of its body. To the head is often added eyes, in the form of beads or painted on in a variety of colours. Whether these eyes make any difference to the fish catching potential of our lure is debatable, but I myself cannot resist painting them on, in the hope that it will make the difference between catching the big one or not, and until someone proves categorically that they do not I shall continue to do so.

And at the end of the fly, where it belongs, we have the tail. Many long winged patterns do not require a tail in their makeup, but those lures that do, utilise the normal kinds of feathers etc. found in conventional flies, slips of red Ibis (substitute) dyed feathers of the swan, duck and goose, strips of various turkeys, bunches of hair, coloured flosses and wools. Many a pattern is enhanced by the use of fluorescent wool as a tag or tail.

That then gives the reader a brief list of the variety of materials one can use for the streamer and bucktail type of lure. The size of fly depends on the species sought, the type and quality of water to be fished. I personally am a believer in the old adage 'Big bait . . . Big fish'. Since using the larger fly my own personal record of fish caught throughout the season has risen by leaps and bounds. Some anglers swear by a two or three hook tandem fly. I must admit that where large fish are to be expected they may well be necessary, or if the creature we are endeavouring to represent by our lure requires the extra length that a combination hook rig gives, then I have no argument against their use, but in the main I prefer a single hook fly. A chapter later in the book is devoted to this double/treble hook lure and examples too are found in the realms of sea angling lures.

HOOKS

Streamer and bucktails are more often than not tied on long shank hooks. There are some patterns however that only require a normal or short shank hook, some of the patterns for sea fishing are such instances. For streamers and bucktail flies for Atlantic salmon fishing normal type salmon fly hooks can be used, the Lowater hook being particularly effective.

The following list of sizes, types, and makes of hook are my own personal choice.

VENIARDS
Longshank Limerick Fine wire   Bronzed
Longshank Limerick Heavy wire Bronzed

Longshank Forged Flat   Bronzed
For Salmon Ordinary Forged Upeyed Black
            Lowater long shank Upeyed Black

MUSTAD
No. 79582 6x Mustad Viking
No. 9124 3x Mustad Sproat
No. 7858 6x Nickel

[2]

The Dressing of Lures and Streamers

It is not the intention of this chapter to instruct the beginner in the art of fly dressing. There are many books available on the subject, and to my mind the best two are by John Veniard: *Fly Dressers Guide*, and *A Further Guide to Fly Dressing*, both published by A. & C. Black Ltd. Those wishing to pursue the subject of fly dressing and to learn this fascinating diversion would do well to buy either of these books and benefit from the wealth of knowledge and techniques that are found in both of them. This chapter is only to pass on a few tips and wrinkles that I personally have found useful and to emphasise a few points that are essential in the construction of good sturdy lures.

There are some streamer patterns that do require a certain amount of skill and expertise in their manufacture, but you can take as a general rule that this type of fly is easier to construct than many others.

Varnish

This is one of the most important elements in fly construction and also one of the least mentioned in works devoted to the art of fly tying. For many years there have been two types of varnish available to the fly dresser. One, the spirit/shellac type of varnish which to my mind has always been a little messy and long drying. Two, the cellulose dope type of varnish which is far easier to use and dries in no time.

What ever varnish you use it has got to be of the right consistency. Too thick and it does not penetrate through the whipping silk to the feathers or hair of the fly's wings, therefore the wings will soon part company with the rest of the fly. Always when you purchase a tin or bottle of varnish make certain you have the appropriate thinners to accompany it, and when not in use always keep the lid or stopper on the tin.

At the time of writing a new varnish has come on to the market and will prove a boon to the dressers of hairwing type flies. E. Veniard Ltd. of Thornton Heath, Surrey are marketing this polyurethane varnish under the name of Venglaze. It has the property of setting rock hard in about ten minutes and is particularly useful in the construction of the Muddler Minnow type flies, when tied with the aid of Venglaze the hair does not pull out.

Winging for Streamers
For the best and neatest wings saddle hackles are the best feathers

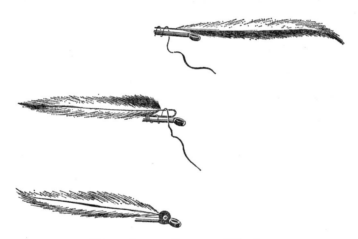

Fig. 5 Reverse Streamer Winging

to use. These saddle hackles are usually more mobile and better formed to provide that fishlike simulation that our streamer flies are all about.

Always match your feathers carefully in relation to one another and to the size of hook you are using so that a neat wing results and the resultant fly is in all-round proportion.

A wing comprising four feathers is a far better wing than a

streamer that is constructed with just two, a certain amount of body is required in a streamer wing and four feathers help to create this; two do not.

Instead of stripping the soft flue from the base of the hackle feather, cut down to about $\frac{1}{16}$ of an inch and at the point of tying-in apply pressure to the stalks with the thumbnail. This short flue helps to retain the wings and there is less chance of the wings pulling out when the fly is subjected to the vigorous casting that is sometimes necessary on the larger day ticket waters.

A method of constructing sturdy non pull-out wings is obtained by applying the wing feathers in reverse, that is to say tied to point over the eye of the hook then turned back and once more tied in to form the head of the fly. (Fig. 5).

Winging for Bucktails

After you have cut off an amount of hair for your bucktails wing discipline yourself and extract a few more hairs from your selected bunch of fur and then you may well have the right amount for the fly's wing. The secret of good bucktails is the sparseness of the dressing; too much hair and the fly loses much of its attraction in the water.

Before tying-in the hair wing soak the roots in Venglaze or any other varnish and, while this is drying, prepare other wings. This wing preparation is useful for flies that incorporate more than one colour in their makeup; a fly such as the Mickey Finn Bucktail having three colour bands. Prepare each portion of coloured bucktail separately, apply the varnish to the roots of each, but before the varnish is quite dry bring the hairwings together, you then will have a wing of three colours, unmixed. Apply these to the hook with a locking hitch, i.e. two turns over the hair, one under and over again.

Jungle Cock Substitutes

As stated in the introductory chapter, the ban on the import of jungle cock feathers leaves a gap in the traditional method of providing our lures and flies with cheeks. Some people maintain that a jungle cock feather does not make one iota of difference to the

killing properties of a fly. That's as may be, they are welcome to
their opinion—but I disagree. I always have confidence when I
fish a fly adorned with this pretty little feather, apart from which if
one claims that fly tying is an art then the result of our labours
must have the ability to catch fish, true, but the flies I feel must
have an aesthetic quality also.

Mention has already been made of the plastic eye feathers and
silver or gold mylar cheeks. When the dressing requires a short
jungle cock feather tied close to the cheek, then it can be dispensed
with altogether, and an eye painted on to the head instead.

A blob of thick white varnish followed by a lateral line in black
can also be used, when applied direct to the side of the wing, but
the varnish must be thick. Ladies white nail varnish is ideal. The
spotted feathers of the more common guinea fowl can be cut to
vaguely simulate the jungle cock feather and would do at a pinch.
All these substitutes can be used to reasonable effect, but I for one
am saddened at the loss of such a beautiful feather, but if it is to
save the species from extinction then it is to the good.

Large feathers off a jungle cock cape, that could only previously
be used for very large salmon flies, can be utilised for much smaller
flies by splitting down the centre, that is providing we possess such
a cape in the first place.

Felt-Tip Pens
There are two types of felt-tip pen on the market, one containing
waterproof ink, the other a washable non-waterproof ink. It goes
without saying you use the former. I only mention this as I made
the mistake once of using the latter. It is now well known that these
pens can be used to make badger and furnace hackles from plain
feathers. Cree effects are obtained in the same way. They can also
be utilised in the formation of bi-coloured feathers for streamer
wings, i.e. a white hackle, the top half marked in with a dark green
ink provides a suitable fish back effect. They are used to provide
lures with spots and irregular markings. Mylar bodies and cheeks
can of course be marked in the same way, with either vertical or
horizontal bands.

Nylon Wools

The modern man-made 'Bri Nylon' type wools make an excellent body medium for some flies. They can be applied either as a dubbing or they can be wound on to provide a bulky body that some patterns call for. These nylon wools are considerably stronger than the natural product.

A visit to your local wool or 'Art and Craft' establishment can often provide a wealth of fly tying materials ranging from coloured lurex to various coloured raffias and raffenes. On one occasion I was able to purchase a tinselled polyester fibre which makes an ideal lure body with its own built-in rib.

The Whip Finish

No fly is complete without a good whip finish. Most competent

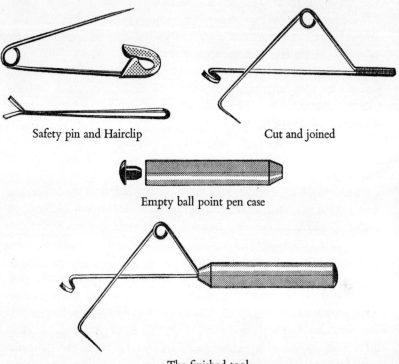

Safety pin and Hairclip   Cut and joined

Empty ball point pen case

The finished tool

Fig. 6   Whip Finish tool

fly dressers find no difficulty in this procedure. I for one am not numbered amongst them and have resorted to a whip finish tool which finishes off my flies far quicker than if I had to resort to using my fingers which take on the guise of thumbs when I normally attempt the whip finish.

Companies that purvey fly tying tools sell amongst them a whip

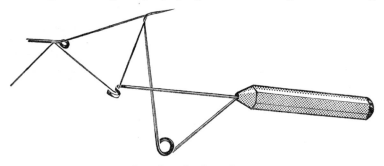

Fig. 7   The whip finish tool in operation

finish tool. Those of you who are of a handy nature can fashion the same quite easily from a large safety pin and a hair clip. The preceding diagrams show this.

Bead Eyes
Some effective flies of the conventional and of the streamer variety make use of this form of adornment. A good source of small coloured beads can be found in the form of the embellishment on some makes of women's hair nets. These nets can be purchased from the usual chain stores and provide the tyer with enough beads to equip enumerable lures with gaudy little beady eyes.

I have found it easier to tie the beads on to a separate piece of silk, wire or nylon as in the following Fig. 8(a) and then tie this 'barbell' on to the head (Fig. 8b).

Stripped Hackles
Mention was made earlier of the use of the felt-tip pen to provide a bi-colour wing. This effect can also be achieved by stripping the outer hackle of the streamer, i.e. leaving a dark olive upper, exposing the white feather of the under saddle hackle and vice versa,

the back of the fish is simulated in this way. (Fig. 9). To provide the fly with a barring effect the outer hackle can be cut as in Fig. 9(b).

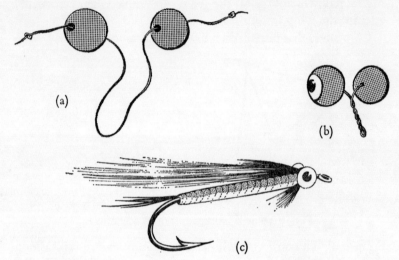

Fig. 8   (a) & (b) Bead optic eyes (c) Optic Bucktail

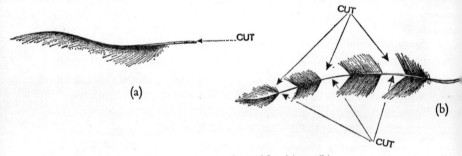

Fig. 9   Stripped Hackles (a) & (b)

Extra Sparkle

Tinsel or wool bodies can often be enhanced by the sparkle glitter powder that one can buy for Christmas decorations. My young daughter had, and I am afraid had is the operative word, small tubes of various colours of this sparkling material. By varnishing the body and applying this powdered tinsel, streamers with a glittering scaly effect are achieved.

Tandem Lures

FIRST ROW.   Grafham Grey Lure (*Saville*)
Tartar (*Norris Shakespeare*) Chew/Blagdon Lure (*Saville*) Mystic (*Norris Shakespeare*)

SECOND ROW. Roach Fry (*Saville*)   Perch Fry (*Saville*)   Green Lure (*Saville*)

THIRD ROW. Hairwing Black Lure   Yellow & Black Lure   Stickleback Lure (*all Sav*

FOURTH ROW. Red Flasher   Claret Lure   Alaska Mary Ann (*all Saville*)

FIFTH ROW. Olive Terror   Greenwell Lure   Black Terror (*all Train*)

SIXTH ROW.   Badger Lure   Yellow Peril   Black Lure

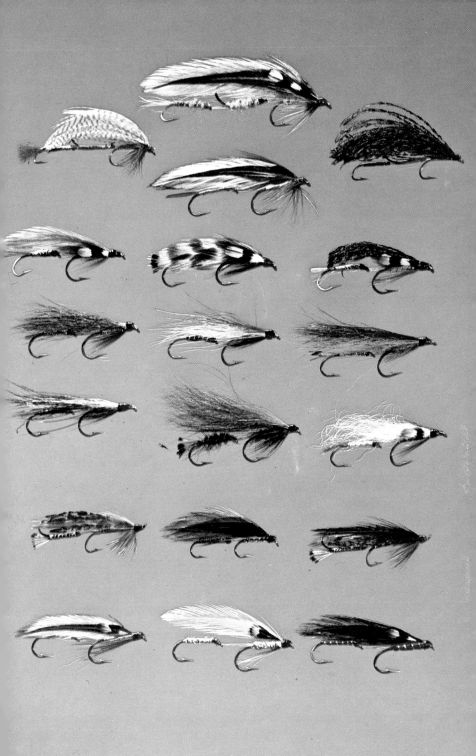

The Weighted Hook

It is often necessary to weight the lure, especially when for use
as a spin fly, for use with a fixed spool/monofilament tackle set-up.
This kind of fly can be fished on its own or as the hook portion of a
spinner fly combination. With conventional fly tackle a weighted
fly is oftimes used to attain depth, usually early in the season.
Sinking lines, both fast and slow, and modern sinktip lines now
make the weighting of the fly superfluous in 90% of the cases.

Where a weighted fly is desired, copper or lead wire is carefully

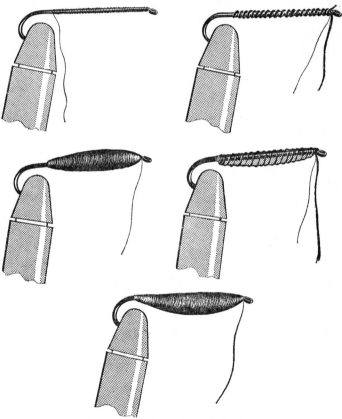

Fig. 10   Weighted Underbody

Tying silk underbody   Lead or copper wire spiral
Floss silk overbody   Lead strip under hook
                     Floss silk overbody

c

spiralled on to the hook shank as per the diagram. A single strip of lead can be tied in under the shank of the hook, again as the diagram, this method being particularly effective when a weighted 'belly' fly such as a plump little perch etc. is desired (Fig. 10).

Weighted Lure Identification
In our fly boxes we could well have both weighted and unweighted lures. A good tip I learnt from some of the professional American fly dressers is to give the weighted fly a different coloured head, i.e. red or white instead of the usual black. Any fly thus marked can be identified as a weighted hook at a glance. This is particularly useful in differentiating between weighted and unweighted lures of the same pattern.

Goldfingering
When a chunky, scintillating body is required I find Goldfingering fits the bill. This material comes in a wide range of shades and provides the fly dresser with an efficient speedy way of providing our lures with flash and glitter, without the tedium of tying a floss underbody. The material is manufactured by H. G. Twilley from Lurex and Courtlands Duracol Viscose. It is readily available in most wool shops. It is shrinkproof and colourfast and is unaffected by the action of salt water; therefore it can be useful in the construction of sea lures.

REFERENCE NUMBERS

WG 5 Silver	WG 2 Gold
WG 7 Silver/Rose	WG 10 Copper
WG 9 Silver/Blue	WG 11 Jade
WG 9 Bronze	WG 12 Pewter

Deer Hair
One of the best ways of colouring clipped deer hair is to resort to using the waterproof felt-tipped pen. The best way to use the same is on the hair after it has been clipped. It is easier, quicker and less messy than attempting to dye the hair before use and, to my mind, the finished result is every way better than the dyed product especially in the darker colours such as black, brown etc.

[3]

Which Streamer to Choose

As with conventional fly patterns the number of streamers the angler has to choose from is legion. Like magpies we hoard pattern after pattern on the advice of angling pundits, shopkeepers and bailiffs or on pure hearsay. Who of us has not heard that on such or such water the only fly to use is the 'Blue Winged Whatsit' or the 'Yellow Bodied So and So'. Arming ourselves with these said patterns we find ourselves fishless after a couple of hours, we wonder at the credibility of the well-meaning advice given to us by a shopkeeper or in the writing of some olympian writer whose piscatorial word is law. After these two hours we may slowly come to the conclusion that either they (the well meaning advisers) are fools and could not possibly catch a fish in a goldfish bowl, or there are no fish left in the water, which incidentally is my excuse for the absence of caught fish and my many blank days. Or do we come to the conclusion that if we used what common sense we are endowed with, we have not been fishing the water correctly with the right kind of fly for the conditions that prevail at the time. Our lures, put on so faithfully on the well meaning advice of others, have probably been bouncing off the noses of the trout, who have shown as much desire to take the same as Mohammedans do for pigs, because the fly's colour is incorrect, the size wrong, and the speed at which we retrieved it not quite right for the conditions. So what lure do we choose? Before selection a look at the water we are about to fish is indeed helpful, and the weather and light conditions at the time most important. Both these points are of equal importance in enabling us to select the right fly that will enhance our catch or make the difference between a good or blank day. So the man who spends the previous evening carefully tying his flies to the cast before appraising the water, must either be optimistic or clairvoyant, or even both.

The fishing capabilities of our streamer or bucktail lures depend on many factors. As stated previously the size of the fly in relation to the water to be fished, and to the size of the quarry we are seeking, is most important. In low clear water for example the fly that is of a small size, quite sparse in its dressing and of the representative type would be the best to use. In coloured or flood water a brighter and larger lure would be more advisable.

What do we need in our lure apart from size? I would say that the following points are all of equal importance. Its aquatic shape —it is all very well dressing a fly at the tying bench thinking that in it we have a killing pattern, without giving thought as to what this fly is going to look like in the water. In the water and, more important, to the fish it has got to have a fishlike shape. Flies that when dry look a bit sparse and motheaten may well, once under water, take on the effective apparel of a small minnow or stickle-back. Similarly a marabou fly that has all the appearance of a feather duster when dry and in the vice, becomes under water a pulsating moving lure full of fish-attracting allure.

After aquatic shape we must consider colour. A choice of what colour lure to choose must depend on the water conditions and light intensity at the time of fishing. At times our streamer must have colours approximating to the natural colouration of the natural fish we are imitating (this is especially true in low clear water conditions when our quarry can see only too well what is offered to it, and vice versa in thick murky conditions a lure that is seen by the fish will catch fish). There is no point in using a fly that has the natural camouflage of a real fish if the water or light is such that the quarry too will fail to see it.

The other two important factors needed by our streamer or bucktail lures are mobility and flash. The mobility comes either in its integral make-up or is imparted by the angler by skilful use of his rod and line retrieve. In most cases the streamer must have that irresistible flash that is so important to its attractiveness and fish catching capabilities. When we watch a shoal of small minnows or fry in the water we see them as small dusky shapes until the sunlight catches one small fish as it turns, then we have a glance at that scintillating flash of its silvery sides. Strips of silvery sunlight caught in our vision for a brief moment, frighten the shoal and for a split second the water shimmers with liquid silver as they dart to safety. This is what the predatory fish see, to them this flash of silver is the sounding of the dinner gong. To them flash means food.

How much of a fly's colour a fish sees is a question that has graced the pages of angling publications and books for a very long time and will do so for many years to come I feel very sure. Theories that trout are colour blind, have a preference for red, blue, green, orange, etc. appear with monotonous regularity. I believe fish do see colour, depending on the depth at which the fly is fished, clarity or opacity of the water, and what is very important the strength and position of the sun in relation to the fly and the fish. If one has swum under water and looked up to the surface any object that is on or near the surface loses most of its colour and appears almost as a silhouette when the sun is bright and shining directly above the object. When the object moves out of direct sunlight it no longer appears so black, and vestiges of colour start to appear. Many eminent authorities maintain that fish are colour blind, I do not feel qualified to disagree, but if fish were colour blind why do some species bedeck themselves in colour at mating times? If they were colour blind the female of the species would notice no difference and the red finery of some fish would pass unnoticed, and it is possible the species would die out through lack of sexual recognition. The deeper the fish lie the less colour they are bound to see. Bearing this in mind, the choice of streamer patterns early in the season is that much easier. As our quarry lie deep down, still affected by the cold and winter torpor we are forced to plumb the depths with our fly. At such depths the question of colour is of little importance and a sombre black lure is as good as any. Research into the record books will probably show a great number of fish were caught on black flies fished deep and slow at the start of the season.

Flies of the black wing variety are usually killing at this time of the year (the 'Black Lure' is one such fly). Others that have been successful for me in the early cold days of March and April are the Black Marabou, Sweeny Todd and Black and Orange Marabou, all of these lures have that silver rib or body that is so important to the fish catching capabilities of our lure.

I always fish a black-winged, or more precisely a dark-winged fly, when fishing deep, in very bright sunlight or at dusk. In order to stir our fish, in this case the trout, from its winter lethargy it is at times necessary to use a fly much larger than one would use later in the season for the same fish. But as the season progresses a step down in size is more productive, so that if early in the season we are forced to use, shall we say, a size 6 or even a size 4 hook, by June a size 8 or 10 would be more appropriate and rewarding, and a change of pattern from the attractor to the more direct representation would be more beneficial.

A knowledge of the indigenous species in the water to be fished is essential in aiding one to dress or choose a fly. In some waters prolific shoals of minnow attract the attention of our trout quarry, yet in other waters stickleback or perch and roach fry form the 'little' fish population that the Rainbow and Brown trout feed on.

Throughout the season I have found that rainbows can be taken on the more bizarre and exotic creations, but the brown trout falls victim to more soberly dressed lures. This may well be due to the fact that the brown trout is a more solitary fish with more time to be selective about its food. The rainbows on the other hand have a tendency to roam in loose shoals and any food that appears is contested for by more than one fish so less time is taken to discriminate and the quickest eats. That is why when a rainbow is caught from a spot it is quite usual to take another fish there quickly provided you have not frightened the rest of the shoal by clumsy fishing. This is not so with the wily old brown trout—he likes to remain alone taking station in his own definitive territory in a river, protected by a boulder or bend but with a steady stream of food brought to it. Catch a good fish from such a spot and another will take its place before long. In still water the cunning browny patrols regularly a portion of the bank that it considers its very own. At feeding times it cruises majestically in its specified territory eating all that takes its fancy, not being rushed into food competition like its rainbow brother.

So you see the choice of the streamer and bucktail fly can depend on the species sought, the time of the year, the position and strength of the sun or its absence, water temperature, depth and clarity, and of course whether the water is a river or stillwater. It is all very well trying to be scientific in making a choice of lure and a logical analysis of all the above-mentioned conditions may well allow you to select the right fly on the day, but there is one fly that we have left out of our scientific choice and it is that lure that for one reason or another works well for us at all times. It has that indefinite quality of catching fish when all other flies have failed. It very rarely lets us down, having for the angler a sympathetic magic. It is possible that having caught fish on this fly in the past on more than one occasion we subconsciously fish the fly with more skill and conviction knowing all the time that the fly at the end of the cast always turns up trumps.

When to fish the streamer or bucktail? The streamer and buck-tail lure can be fished throughout the season, regardless of temperature and water conditions. However, we would be foolish to fish them to the exclusion of all other types of fly. Who of us does not enjoy fishing with a minute dry fly carefully casting to the rise of a trout at the far bank? Or who does not enjoy manipulating a team of nymphs or buzzers on the appropriate occasion? When all other methods have failed bring out the streamer. Though not the complete panacea to fishless days it may well make the difference between a straight rod and one that bends and throbs in a pulsating arc as a large trout seeks its freedom. After all that is why we go fishing—to catch fish. An angler to my mind is the better for being the complete all-rounder than just a dry fly specialist or a nymph addict. I have nothing against a so-called purist, but let's catch fish by all means without the dogma of narrow minded purism that has always bedevilled angling with flies since fly fishing became a sport. After all the very smallest nymph and dry fly is nothing more than a lure.

Early Season Flies
Black Lures, Black Marabou, Black and Orange Marabou, Sweeny Todd, Painted Lady Streamer, Black Muddler and any fly of a dark nature with plenty of flash. Sizes 4, 6, 8.

May onwards
A step down in size and a change of type of fly now becomes necessary. There is still a need for the flasher type of fly with a touch of red or orange, for at this time of the year the minnow and stickleback bedeck themselves in their mating finery. On the other hand smaller more soberly dressed exact or impressionistic flies start to come into their own. Minnow Streamer, Banded Squirrel Bucktail, Church Fry, Perch Fry Streamer, Muddler Minnow, Orange Streamer, Hairy Bucktail Minnow, Dunkeld Streamer, Alexandra Streamer, Royal Coachman Streamer or Bucktail etc., etc. Sizes 8, 10, 12.

Flood Water or Cloudy Water
Conditions such as these necessitate the use of larger flies around size 6. In cloudy water or murky light the Black Lure comes into its own once more, and by black lure I mean the great variety of dark flies we have at our disposal. It will also pay to ring the changes with yellow, orange or white winged flies. The Black Ghost, Orange or Yellow Muddlers, Yellow Matuka are just a few that have killed fish for me when the water has been the colour of a mild curry. In cloudy water conditions the large fly is necessary for the fish to see the lure and in such conditions the fish are on the look out and are usually less selective in their choice of food.

Low Water and Clear Conditions
This is the most difficult of fish taking times. Due to the crystal clarity of the water our quarry can easily distinguish between an artificial or natural fly or fry. It is therefore common sense that a lure tied to represent the natural fish of the locale such as the millers thumb, or the loach that abound in some waters. Minnow or stickleback representations will serve equally well should they be indigenous to the area we are about to fish. I have seen six-inch

Devon trout choking on a three-inch bullhead in water that was gin-clear. The spiny bullhead is considered fine fare by many species of fish. I have had good trout and chub by fishing a natural bullhead so there is no reason why the Muddler-type bullhead should not do equally as well. For dusk fishing for trout, or on the darkest night when we are out after the shy sea trout, any streamer or bucktail that incorporates a touch of fluorescent material in its construction usually does quite well. The fluorescent medium can be added as tails or as a ribbing medium. If the fly we are fishing has a dubbed wool or fur body some fluorescent material can be worked in with the dubbing.

[4]

Snag-free Fishing

How often do we get snagged or pick up weed when fishing deep? This problem occurs only too often but can be more or less eradicated at the fly bench, as can the problem of hooking up on lily pads or the opposite bank etc. The fact that I lost more flies and casts on over-hanging trees and bushes prompted me to tie flies in the first place, as I found that the ostensibly free fishing on the Welsh mountain streams was costing a small fortune in lost shop-bought flies.

One of the old methods of combating week pick-up was to place a small treble hook higher up the cast in an effort to prevent the weed catching the actual fly. The only trouble with this was that one spent a lot of time taking weed off the treble before making the next cast so the purpose of using this treble was defeating the object.

There is nothing worse than removing weed from flies and, worse still, getting caught up on the tougher varieties of aquatic

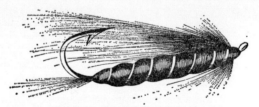

Fig. 11 Upside down Lure

vegetation. Apart from the annoying break in the casting rhythm, a fly masked in weed or snagged on a tough lily root is not catching you fish.

Good fish-holding areas around weed beds are often ignored by anglers for fear of snagging: once bitten twice shy appears to be their motto. They give them a miss, deeming the risk of snagging too great, so they move on to more accessible waters, perhaps leaving behind under the shadow of the lilies a fat bellied monster of a trout whose prodigious size is due solely to the fact that the lilies have sheltered him from the anglers' depredations. The insect and small fish life that abound around weeds have provided him with a rich larder and allowed him to grow lazily fat.

The simplest way of tying a weed-free streamer or any other fly for that matter is to tie the fly in reverse. Every amateur fly dresser claims to invent this fly. This upside-down dressing lends itself far better to the hairwing type of lure rather than the feathered streamer. It does not ride well in the water when retrieved but it does cut down a considerable amount of weed, and the occasional snag up (Fig. 11).

Fig. 12 Nylon Filament

Another method is to introduce a filament of stiffish nylon when dressing the fly. This nylon monofilament comes around the bend of the hook and is tied in at the head. Fig. 12 is an example of this form of weed-free, snag-free lure. E. Veniard Ltd. of Thornton Heath sell a range of these nylon filaments for all sizes of hooks.

A similar method to the last is the one that utilises a fine spring wire loop as in Fig. 13. As you can see, this fine stiff wire is looped down from the head and rests on the point of the hook before the barb. As far as I know this form of hook is unobtainable in this country. The Eagle Claw Company of Denver, Colorado U.S.A. supply a whole range of this type of hook for the purpose of making bass lures. A similar form of weedguard is utilised in some forms of commercial spinners and other metallic lures.

A fourth method is a new innovation in hook design called the Keel Hook. This patented hook is sold by the Keel Hook Fly

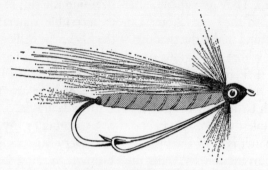

Fig. 13   Wire Loop

Company Inc., a subsidiary of McClelland Industries of Traverse City, Michigan, U.S.A. (Fig. 14). The principle involved can easily be seen in the diagram. It rides over any weed patch, or bounces out of the way of any snag. The centre of gravity of the fly is lowered, therefore the fly will ride correctly on retrieve. The dressing is of course upside down, but its performance as a fly is in no way impaired by this. The first reference to this hook was made in the well known American publication *Field and Stream* in April 1969. Since that time mention has been made in the British

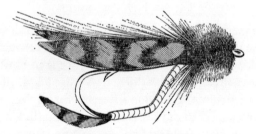

Fig 14. Keel Fly Muddler

press and it will not be long before the hook and tackle wholesalers in this country will list 'Keel' hooks in their catalogues. I have used this form of lure this season, samples of which were kindly sent by the Keel Fly Company. The unusual position of the bite of the hook in no way hinders the hooking capabilities of the lure.

[5]

Mylar and its Uses

Mention has been made of Mylar in earlier chapters as a medium in the construction of streamer and bucktail lures. This is a comparatively new material available on the market for the last three years or so. It is supplied by the two leading fly tying material suppliers, Veniards and Saville, in both sheet and tube form. Mylar came to the notice of American fly dressers in the early 1960s, and since that time more and more patterns have been evolved incorporating this flash and glittering material as a body medium and a great number of both fresh and saltwater lures utilise the flat Mylar strip as an embellishment, in the form of cheeks. Originally this material, like the better known 'Lurex', was created for uses far removed from the manufacture of flies. The silver and gold piping of ceremonial robes or uniforms etc., the iridescence of a shimmering ball gown, are the original uses for which Mylar was created. A form of Mylar is also used as a protective layer in the equipment of America's lunar astronauts. It did not take long however for fly dressers to see a good thing, and now many patterns that used the old tarnishable tinsels make use of this easy to apply, non-tarnish material.

Mylar lends itself better to streamer and bucktail flies than their smaller cousins, standard wet flies. It is a bold material and suits the large, bold lures that we are dealing with in this book.

It is available in the U.S.A. in thread form down to 1/64th of an inch. This fine Mylar strip is extremely useful in the construction of wings for both fresh and salt water lures, providing that extra flash and glitter to the wings instead of to the body or cheeks of the fly. Mixed with the hair of the wing it provides a shimmering simulation of a fish's body which larger fish find irresistible to the point of madness. This narrow strip is not available as yet in this country, but I felt it worth mentioning as this form of Mylar,

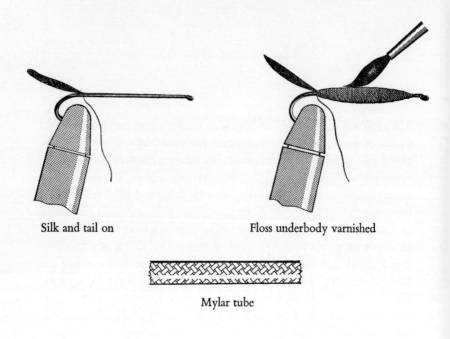

Silk and tail on   Floss underbody varnished

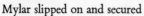

Mylar tube

Mylar slipped on and secured   The finished lure

Fig. 15   Mylar Bodied Lures

being fine, does not hamper casting and does not cause the flutter that Mylar cheeks do, giving air resistance that lessens our casting distance. To obtain fine strands of Mylar for winging purposes it is possible to shave fine strips from the flat sheet or to carefully unpick some of the Mylar tubing into its individual strands. Both these methods are a little laborious, but if one can catch the fish of one's dreams all the labour would be worthwhile.

Mylar Tubing

This form of Mylar has a cotton core running through its centre. The reason for this is as stated earlier that its prime purpose was in the manufacture of piping for uniforms etc. This cotton core has to be removed before it can be utilised for the manufacture of lure bodies. The removal of the core is easy as it is not attached in any way to the outer Mylar. Before applying the Mylar to the hook, an underbody of floss silk must be built up, and a strand of tying silk left at the tail. A liberal coating of clear varnish is then applied and the Mylar slipped on whilst still wet. If the pattern of fly calls for a tail this of course must be tied in before building up the underbody. The tail end of the Mylar is then tied in and trimmed or left untrimmed if extra flash is desired. The head end is then finished off and the usual procedures for winging and hackles carried out.

By using felt-tipped pens the plain gold or silver Mylar can be transformed into a multi-coloured striped or banded body, and a coating of clear varnish applied overall, not only to protect the colouring but also to extend the life of the fly from the sharp teeth of our fish adversaries. The diagrams in Fig. 15 clarify the whole procedure of applying Mylar tubing.

Multi-hook lures can be treated in the same way or the linkage alone can be covered by the Mylar tube, giving that extra flash to our tandem lure.

Mylar Cheeks

These flat Mylar cheeks can be an added attraction to the fish-catching streamer. The application of these cheeks is a simple matter indeed as the illustration shows—just two strips tied either side of the fly in a size to suit the size of hook used. For size 8 long-shank hooks a strip about ⅛ inch will be adequate, with correspondingly wider strips for larger hooks. Some sea lures use strips up to ½ in to ¾ in wide.

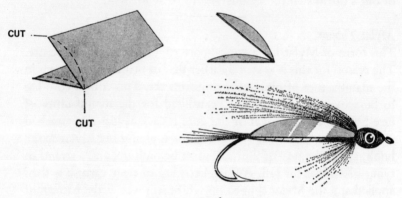

Fig. 16   Mylar Strip

The following four flies incorporate the flat Mylar cheeks or the Mylar tubing body. These are of course American patterns and are to be found in the vast range of patterns supplied by Orvis Company Inc. of Manchester, Vermont.

These dressings have caught both rainbow and brown trout for me, and are based on the flies of Bob Zwirz of Connecticut, U.S.A.

Mylar Silver Shiner Bucktail

TAIL.   White bucktail.
BODY.   White wool.
WING.   White bucktail Olive bucktail over.
CHEEK.   Silver Mylar strip either side.
HEAD.   Black white painted eye black pupil.

This fly is also dressed as the original but with marabou feathers rather than bucktail, and an olive and white under-wing can be added.

Mylar Bodied Silver Shiner Bucktail

TAIL. None.

BODY. Silver Mylar tubing.

HACKLE. A few fibres of short scarlet cock, spike hackle.

WING. White bucktail, dark blue or black bucktail over.

HEAD. Black, white eye black pupil.

Mylar Golden Shiner Bucktail

TAIL. Yellow bucktail.

BODY. Pale yellow wool or fur.

HACKLE. Orange cock fibres tied as spike.

WING. Yellow bucktail, olive bucktail over.

CHEEK. Gold Mylar strip.

HEAD. Black, yellow eye black pupil.

As in the silver shiner, marabou feathers can be used instead of bucktail.

Mylar Bodied Mickey Finn

TAIL. None.

BODY. Silver bodied Mylar tubing, the tail whippings varnished red. (All Orvis patterns have this).

WING. Yellow bucktail, red over, then yellow bucktail.

CHEEK. Jungle cock tied short.

HEAD. Black.

The original dressings for the above mentioned flies are to be found in that excellent book, *Streamer Fly Tying and Fishing* by Colonel Joseph D. Bates Jnr. and published by Stackpole Books. This book is available now in this country and anyone wishing to obtain the original dressings of some 300 streamer and bucktail flies would do well to purchase the same. It truly is an authoritative work on the subject.

Two other types of lures that can be tied using Mylar tubing, though not of the streamer or bucktail family, are worth mentioning if only to show the versatility of this body medium.

The first is the Jersey Herd Mylar bodied in Gold. The dressing for this was given in John Veniard's book *Reservoir and Lake Flies*

D

(A. & C. Black). It is a coincidence that it is mentioned there, for I can truly say that I was one of the first customers of his to purchase the Mylar tubing from him. The first fly I tied with this material was in fact the Jersey Herd.

Mylar Jersey Herd. (Further dressings of the herd family are given in a later chapter).

>   TAIL AND BACK.   Bronze peacock herl tied in at the tail and carried across the back.
>   BODY.   Gold Mylar.
>   HACKLE.   Orange.
>   HEAD.   Peacock herl.

The next fly I had to tie was a special for a client of mine. Its purpose was as a static lure, a type of fly that is allowed to rest on the bottom and tempt those extra large trout that forage on the muddy bottom. I am not a lover of this form of fly fishing, but there are those who advocate this as a method of taking trout from large reservoirs.

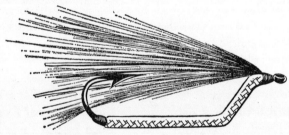

Fig. 17 Integration (Keel Fly Co.)

Mylar Bodied Static Fly

>   TAIL.   Magenta fluorescent wool.
>   BODY.   Silver Mylar tubing, two turns of fluorescent magenta wool behind front hackle.
>   HACKLES.   Both black cock stiff in fibre, one at the head, one at the tail.
>   HEAD.   Black.

A number of flies sent to me by the Keel Fly Company at Traverse City, Michigan incorporate in the dressing the fine Mylar in the hair of the wings as well as in the tubing of the body. The two patterns given are tied ostensibly for salt water fishing.

Bonesnook Special (Keel Fly Co.)

TAIL.   None.

BODY.   Silver Mylar.

WING.   White bucktail, then yellow bucktail over, then white once more with strands of narrow flat Mylar interspersed throughout the hair.

HEAD.   Red.

Integration (Keel Fly Co.)

TAIL.   None.

BODY.   Silver Mylar tubing.

WING.   White bucktail, then black bucktail over. Mylar strands interspersed throughout.

HEAD.   Red.

[6]

The Muddlers

If some superior being ordained that from henceforth I was only to use one pattern of fly for all my fishing I would have no hesitation in choosing the Muddler Minnow in all sizes. It is the nearest thing to a 'magic' fly that mortals have created to catch fish. This 'Merlin' concoction of deer-hair and feather has the property of being all things to all fish, apparently changing its appearance and having universal appeal to many species of fresh and saltwater fish. It can simulate a small fish, a grasshopper, a nymph, a beetle larva, a cricket, a mayfly or stone fly, a shrimp, or prawn, and even a skittering sedge. This fly has caught all species of trout, salmon and seatrout in this country. Both pike and perch have fallen to the allure of the Muddler whilst in the country of its origin bass, crappies, walleyes and many other indigenous fresh water and sea-fish of the United States have succumbed to this bundle of deer hair.

Dan Gapen of the Gapen Tackle Company of Anoka, Minnesota tied this fly to represent the cockatush minnow, a species of small fish that is common to the Nipogen river and other eastern waters of North America. Mr. Gapen himself admits that though having this small fish in mind when creating the Muddler, the fact that the original Muddler is of a sombre browny colour, it makes an excellent impression of a nymph.

Since the original fly made its presence felt a host of mutant variations have come on the scene, whether or not these varieties are as good as the original is debatable, but I have had fish on many of them and any fly is worth giving a try if only for fun.

The dressing of the Muddler has been given in many books

since its conception, the first company to retail this fly in the British Isles was Tom Saville Ltd. of Beeston, Notts., who imported the famous fly from the Gapen Tackle Company in 1967.

The Muddler Minnow (Gapen)

TAIL. Oak Turkey strip.

BODY. Gold tinsel (flat) ribbed with gold wire in larger sizes.

WING. Grey squirrel flanked by oak turkey strips tied upright.

HEAD. Spun and clipped deer hair.

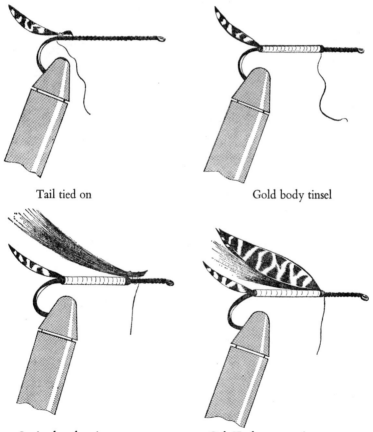

Tail tied on   Gold body tinsel

Squirrel underwing   Oak Turkey overwing

Fig. 18   The Muddler Minnow

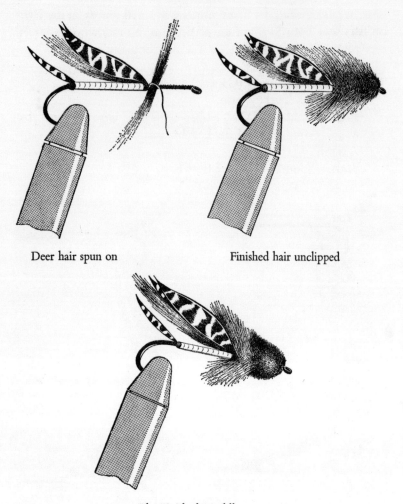

Deer hair spun on   Finished hair unclipped

The Finished Muddler

Fig. 18 (cont.)   The Muddler Minnow

Instead of squirrel, the black bucktail is sometimes used, also
Impala tail has been given as the winging medium in some
publications. To this original Muddler, Dan Gapen has added to
his repertoire with three other Muddlers, the Polar Bear, Yellow
Bear and the Black Bear. As their names suggest they utilise the

guard hairs of the bear family as the winging medium and re
tied in the same way as the original.

Yellow Muddler (As tied by the Orvis Company of Vermont).
    TAIL. A strip of dyed yellow turkey.
    BODY. Flat gold tinsel.
    WING. Bucktail or squirrel flanked by oak turkey strips dyed
      yellow.
    HEAD. Spun and clipped deer hair.

I have another Muddler version in my possession tied by the
Keel Fly Company of Traverse City, Michigan. Apart from the
normal Muddler dressing they have another which incorporates
a peacock herl egg sac.

Muddler Minnow (as tied by the Keel Fly Co. on Keel Weedless
Hooks).
    TAIL. Oak turkey strip.
    BODY. Gold tinsel.
    TAG. An 'egg sac' of green peacock herl.
    WING. Oak turkey, bucktail in between (the pattern I have
      utilised white bucktail).
    HEAD. Clipped deer hair.

Two Muddler-type flies I have tied, and had considerable success with, dispense entirely with the oak turkey strips and rely
entirely on the bucktail wing. Both these flies have proved killing
in flood water conditions.

The Orange Muddler
    TAIL. None.
    BODY. Gold tinsel, gold ribbed.
    WING. Orange bucktail.
    HEAD. Spun and clipped deer hair (leaving some hairs un-
      clipped as a collar).

The Yellow Muddler

TAIL. None.
BODY. Silver tinsel silver ribbed.
WING. Yellow bucktail.
HEAD. Spun and clipped deer hair (as above).

Another Muddler variation I use instead of conventional black lures is the Black Muddler.

The Black Muddler

TAIL. A strip of black swan.
BODY. Black floss silver silk rib.
WING. Black bucktail or black squirrel flanked by black swan wing.
HEAD. Black chenille (built up large and bulky like the deer hair heads).

The famous angler and author Richard Walker devised the following Muddler variations which are retailed by the well-known fly fishing company Tom Saville Ltd. The heads of all three flies are somewhat longer than the normal Muddler.

Black Muddler (Walker)

TAIL. None.
BODY. Black floss fine oval silver rib.
WING. Black squirrel.
HEAD. Spun and clipped deer hair.

Black and White Muddler (Walker)

TAIL. None.
BODY. Scarlet floss silk, fine oval silver rib.
WING. Mixed black and white bucktail.
HEAD. Spun and clipped deer hair.

Texas Rose Muddler (Walker)

TAIL. None.
BODY. Orange floss silk, fine oval silver rib.

WING. Yellow bucktail.

HEAD. Spun and clipped deer hair.

The following simple Muddler has proved particularly effective for rainbow trout and I have friends who prefer to fish with this fly to the exclusion of other Muddler patterns.

Red Squirrel Muddler

BODY. Red lurex (varnished with three coats of varnish for durability).

WING. Red Squirrel fibres (natural).

HEAD. Spun and clipped deer hair.

Another of Dan Gapen's flies I have used for Rainbow Trout is the Thief. Originally tied for both trout and other panfish of the U.S.A., it does remarkably well in this country when a dark fly is required with plenty of silver flash. Tied in larger sizes I visualise this as a good pattern for pike. In the smaller sizes many perch have been taken on this little flasher.

The Thief (Gapen)

TAIL. Red swan or goose strip.

BODY. Silver tinsel.

WING. Grey squirrel flanked by oak turkey strips set upright.

HEAD. Black chenille (tied full and bulky).

Two small fish of the British Isles that are easily represented by the Muddler conception are the miller's thumb or bullhead and the lowly loach. I have taken both brown and rainbow trout on these two flies whenever I have used them.

Loach Muddler

BODY. Hare's fur ribbed wide, oval tinsel (gold).

WING. Four dyed brown Plymouth rock hackles extending well beyond the hook.

UNDER WING (Hackle). White bucktail.

HEAD. Spun and clipped deer hair that has previously been dyed olive brown.

This fly is enhanced by the addition of two small Jungle cock feathers tied in at the head and pressed into the deer hair.

Fig. 19   Miller's Thumb Muddler

The Miller's Thumb

BODY.   Hare's fur and green seal's fur mixed, ribbed with wide oval gold tinsel.

WING.   Brown bucktail or squirrel flanked by dyed brown/ olive grizzle hackles.

CHEEKS.   Three feathers from either a pheasant or grouse, depending on whether a dark or light representation is required. Two of the feathers are tied in behind the head, on the outside of the hackle wings, the third is tied flat on top of the fly to give the impression of the broad flat head of the Bullhead.

HEAD.   Clipped deer hair dyed brown and mixed with natural undyed hair.

A similar pattern to the above is an American pattern tied to represent a similar species of broad headed minnow common to some waters in the States, this is the Sculpin Minnow.

The next two patterns are just a couple of examples of a new range of muddler type flies utilising the very mobile marabou feather as a winging medium. By ringing the changes in colour of the marabou wing a host of patterns could be evolved, but to my mind the black-winged variety is far and away the most effective. Why trout take such a weird looking object I do not know, but they do.

In the American versions the body is constructed out of a Christmas tinsel. However, by using a wool base heavily lacquered and liberally coated with the glitter powder mentioned in the chapter on the tying of streamers, a very attractive chunky body with lots of flash is achieved.

Black Marabou Muddler
TAIL. Red Ibis or swan.
BODY. Silver tinsel glitter quite full.
WING. Black marabou, with a few strands of bronze peacock over.
HEAD. Spun and clipped deer hair.

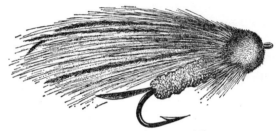

Fig. 20   Marabou Muddler

White Marabou Muddler
TAIL. Red Ibis or dyed swan.
BODY. Silver tinsel glitter.
WING. White marabou strands of peacock over.
HEAD. Spun and clipped deer hair.

Other colours that are used: Red, Brown, Brown and White, Grey and Green.

As you can see the range of Muddlers is on the increase and I feel sure we have not seen an end to the variations and patterns, all incorporating the large head which is the trade mark as it were of the Muddler Family.

The Muddler Minnow can be fished at all speeds and at all depths. Weighted and slowly retrieved along the bottom is one particularly effective method of taking fish. Another is when the fly is retrieved in the surface film quite quickly so that a wake is formed. Fish are often noted following the fly in before the take.

Other examples of Muddler type flies are to be found in the chapter on Additional Patterns.

[7]

The Multi-Hook Lures

For Trout and Salmon
The reasons for the use of a multi-hook combination fly are (1) its use when large fish are anticipated and (2), when the lure is tied to represent a creature whose size necessitates a long-winged simulation.

These tandem hooks come in a variety of different combinations:

Two hook: both turned down, and it is usual to have the front hook two sizes larger than the rear, i.e. size 8 front hook size 10 back.
Two hook: one up, one down.
Three hook: all down.
Three hook: front down, middle up, rear hook down.
One single hook front, rear hook a double hook.
Front hook single, rear hook treble.
And so forth.

The linkage between the hooks can be of nylon, single strand and of reasonable strength (say 15 lbs breaking strain), twisted double or treble strands of nylon, or standard strengths of wire trace either bare or coated in plastic. There are conflicting schools of thought as to which is the better linkage, wire or nylon. Some maintain that the nylon is susceptible to deterioration and to eventual kinking. The other school of thought prefers the suppleness of nylon and abhors the rigidity of the wire linkage. So it becomes a question of paying your money and taking your pick, and those of you who tie your own flies can choose for yourself and try both linkages, bearing in mind the quarry that you are ultimately seeking when you gauge the strength of the linking wire or nylon.

The following patterns are of traditional design, modern reservoir lures tied for reservoir fishing, or for the larger cousins of the trout, the seatrout and salmon. Where known the originators or suppliers of the lures are given. In compiling this book I received many dressings from individual fly dressers and commercial concerns.

As with other types of fly, flies that were originally tied for a specific water can prove equally killing on distant lakes or rivers far removed from the water on which the fly was conceived. An example of this is the Grafham Lure. This is a lure that, as the name suggests, was tied with the vast man-made lake in mind, to tempt the large brown and rainbow trout. It killed 16 salmon on Lough Corrib in Ireland. So you see it pays to be ambitious and experimental in your approach to fly selection, and not be strangled by quaint and old fashioned dogma. Do not be conservative if a little voice says try so-and-so—go ahead and use it. So what if the fly has never been used on the particular water. Ignore the jibes—go ahead and catch fish, for the very fact that you have confidence in the fly means you will fish the better. Listen and endure the comments and laughter of your friends, but listen further to the tune changing when you proceed to catch fish, and do not be surprised if they beg a pattern from you. It has happened to me. In one afternoon I converted a dry fly purist and a wet fly expert to the Muddler Minnow on a day when the difficult fish craved for the deer hair fly and ignored other lures of feathers on and below the surface. He who laughs last more often than not laughs longest.

Alexandra Lure
TAIL.   Red Ibis and green peacock sword herl.
BODY.   Flat silver tinsel, oval silver rib.
Front Hook
BODY.   Silver tinsel, silver rib as rear hook.
HACKLE.   Black hen.
WING.   Green peacock herl flanked by long strips of red swan or goose.

Jungle Alexandra

Dressing as above pattern except for the addition of jungle cock cheeks either side of the wing.

Dunkeld Lure

This lure like the Alexandra is one of the lures derived from the traditional wet fly. This lure has proved its worth on many of the new reservoirs.

TAIL.   Golden pheasant crest.

BODY.   Gold tinsel gold oval rib.

Front Hook

BODY.   Gold tinsel gold rib as rear hook.

HACKLE.   Hot orange.

WING.   Brown mallard flank.

CHEEKS.   Jungle cock.

Black Lure—1

Perhaps one of the most popular reservoir lures in use today, this fly has taken both brown and rainbow trout on all reservoirs in the country. There are many variations of this particular fly, the following dressings are just a few that I personally have been asked to tie at various times:

TAIL.   None.

BODY.   Black floss silk ribbed silver wire.

Front Hook

BODY.   Black floss silk silver rib.

HACKLE.   Black hen.

WINGS.   Four black saddle hackles.

Black Lure—2

TAIL.   None.

BODY.   Black floss silver rib.

Front Hook

BODY.   Black floss silver rib.

HACKLE.   Black hen.

WING.   Four black saddle hackles Bronze peacock herl over.

Black Lure—3

Dressing as for No. 1 with the addition of jungle cock cheeks.

Black Lure—4

Dressing as for No. 3 with the addition of a red fluorescent tail.

Jungle Cock Lure

    TAIL. Golden pheasant tippets.
    BODY. Silver tinsel silver rib.

Front Hook

    BODY. As rear hook.
    HACKLE. Black.
    WING. Two large jungle cock eye feathers back to back.

Teal and Blue Lure

This lure is an adaptation of the smaller teal blue and silver, and like the wet fly, is a good lure for the migratory trout.

    TAIL. Golden pheasant tippets.
    BODY. Flat silver tinsel silver rib.

Front Hook

    BODY. Silver tinsel and rib as above.
    HACKLE. Light blue.
    WING. Barred teal feather.

Teal and Yellow

    TAIL. Golden pheasant tippets.
    BODY. Yellow wool silver rib.

Front Hook

    BODY. Yellow wool silver rib.
    HACKLE. Yellow.
    WING. Barred teal flank.

This last lure is sometimes tied with a gold body and gold rib instead of the yellow wool or fur.

Black and Silver

    TAIL. Red wool or Ibis strip.
    BODY. Silver tinsel silver rib.

Front Hook
- BODY. Silver tinsel silver rib.
- HACKLE. Black.
- WING. Four black saddle hackles.

Black and Gold
Dressing as for Black and Silver and as the name suggests the body is gold.

Kingfisher Lure
- TAIL. Blue kingfisher feather fibres or cock hackle of similar colour.
- BODY. Gold tinsel.

Front Hook
- BODY. Gold tinsel.
- HACKLE. None.
- WING. Orange saddle hackles flanked by two strips of dyed blue swan feather.
- CHEEK. Jungle cock.

Red Terror
- TAIL. Red wool (fluorescent if required).
- BODY. Flat silver tinsel silver rib optional.

Front Hook
- BODY. As rear hook.
- WING. Red hackles flanked by two strips of swan dyed red, strands of green peacock herl over.

Blue Terror
- TAIL. Red wool (fluorescent if required).
- BODY. Flat silver tinsel rib optional.

Front Hook
- BODY. As rear hook.
- WING. Two blue cock hackles flanked by strips of grey drake.

Badger Lure
- TAIL. None.
- BODY. Orange floss silver wire rib.

Front Hook
>   BODY. Orange floss silver rib.
>   WING. Four badger hackles.
>   CHEEK. Jungle cock.

Badger Demon
>   TAIL. Red Ibis, or dyed swan.
>   BODY. Flat silver tinsel.

Front Hook
>   BODY. As rear hook.
>   HACKLE. Red cock.
>   WING. Four badger hackles.

Two flies sent to me by Messrs. Norris Shakespeare Ltd., of Redditch are the Mystic and the Tartar, the dressings are as follows:

Mystic
>   TAIL. None.
>   BODY. Silver (flat).

Front Hook
>   BODY. As rear hook.
>   HACKLE. None.
>   WING. Peacock heil from sword feather.

Tartar
>   TAIL. Red wool.
>   BODY. Flat silver tinsel.
>   HACKLE. Dark blue hackle.
>   WING. Grey mallard flank.

The following traditional pattern for which there are two dressings is one of the flies used for seatrout and salmon which has come back into use on our larger reservoirs for rainbow trout.

Yellow Peril—1
>   TAIL. None.
>   BODY. Silver tinsel, silver wire rib.

E

Front Hook
> BODY. As rear hook.
> HACKLE. Yellow.
> WING. Yellow dyed swan or goose, Golden pheasant toppings over.

Yellow Peril—2
> TAIL. None.
> BODY. Yellow seal fur silver rib.

Front Hook
> BODY. As rear hook.
> HACKLE, Yellow.
> WING. Four yellow hackles.

Jungle cock cheeks are sometimes added, but are not essential.

The following three lures are again traditional seatrout lures that have successfully made the transition to our inland waters for large browns and rainbow trout.

Crested Mallard
> TAIL. None.
> BODY. Flat tinsel silver oval rib.

Front Hook
> BODY. As rear hook.
> HACKLE. None.
> WING. Brown mallard flank golden pheasant topping over.

This particular fly, the Mary Ann, is just a fancy version of the Alexandra.

Mary Ann
> TAIL. None.
> BODY. Flat gold tinsel, gold wire rib.

Front Hook
> BODY. As rear hook.
> HACKLE. None.
> WING. Green peacock sword feather, golden pheasant topping with red dyed swan sides.

Connon
TAIL. Red wool or Ibis feather.
BODY. Flat silver tinsel, silver oval rib.
Front Hook
BODY. As rear hook.
HACKLE. None.
WING. Well marked badger hackles (I prefer to use four).

It will be noticed that the Connon Lure is virtually the Badger Demon minus the hackle, and is included for reference sake. This particular lure, as the name suggests, is used for seatrout in the Connon river estuary.

Red Dandy
TAIL. None.
BODY. Oval silver tinsel.
Front Hook
BODY. As rear hook.
HACKLE. Bright red cock.
WING. Grey mallard flank.

There is also a Blue Dandy, the only difference being the colour of the hackle which, as the name suggests, is a dyed blue.

The well known firm of Tom Saville of Beeston, Notts. supplied me with the following modern reservoir lures which have taken many fish in the waters after which they are named.

The Grafham Grey Lure (Saville)
TAIL. Golden pheasant crest.
BODY. Grey wool or fur, silver rib.
Front Hook
BODY. As rear hook.
HACKLE. Badger hackle.
WING. Two badger hackles.
CHEEK. Jungle cock.

The Chew/Blagdon Lure (Saville)
TAIL. Red dyed swan fibres.
BODY. Flat silver tinsel.

Front Hook
>   BODY.   As rear hook.
>   HACKLE.   Brown.
>   WINGS.   Badger hackles.

The Eyebrook Lure (Saville)
>   TAIL.   None.
>   BODY.   Black floss silk, silver rib.

Front Hook
>   BODY.   As rear hook.
>   HACKLE.   Black.
>   WING.   Badger hackles.

Further examples from this leading fly tackle company to be found in their catalogue are:

Green Lure
>   TAIL.   Red and yellow fluorescent silk.
>   BODY.   Embossed silver tinsel.

Front Hook
>   BODY.   Fluorescent green wool, silver rib.
>   HACKLE.   Red.
>   WING.   Green peacock sword.
>   CHEEK.   Jungle cock.

Red Flasher
>   TAIL.   Red fluorescent floss.
>   BODY.   Red lurex, silver rib.

Front Hook
>   BODY.   As rear hook.
>   HACKLE.   Red.
>   WING.   Badger hair or skunk tail.

The fry of the roach and perch which figure quite highly on the trout's menu are represented by the next two Saville lures in the tandem hook form.

Perch Fry Lure (Saville)
TAIL. Golden pheasant tippets.
BODY. Embossed silver tinsel.
Front Hook
BODY. As rear hook.
HACKLE. Red cock.
WING. Cree hackles.
CHEEK. Jungle cock.

Roach Fry (Saville)
TAIL. Red hackle fibres.
BODY. Embossed silver tinsel.
Front Hook
BODY. As rear hook.
HACKLE. Olive green cock.
WING. Olive green hackles.
CHEEK. Jungle cock.

The following three lures were published in Saville's catalogue in a short list of fluorescent fly patterns.

The White Ghost
TAIL. Golden pheasant tippets.
BODY. White fluorescent chenille silver rib.
Front Hook
BODY. As rear hook.
HACKLE. Black.
WING. White calf tail or ringcat.

Brown and Gold Lure
TAIL. Chrome fluorescent floss.
BODY. Embossed silver tinsel.
Front Hook
BODY. As rear hook.
HACKLE. Orange.
WING. Brown bucktail.

Hairwing Black Lure
TAIL. Blue fluorescent floss.
BODY. Black floss, silver rib.
Front Hook
BODY. As rear hook.
HACKLE. Black.
WING. Black bucktail squirrel or bear.

In compiling this book I sought the help of many fly dressers, one of those who helped me by contributing information and patterns was David Train of Stratton St. Margaret, Near Swindon, Wiltshire. The following list of lures are his. Mr. Train dresses most of his tandem lures by inverting the rear hook. The first two lures, Train's Terror, and Black & Olive, were primarily tied to take fish in Wroughton reservoir near Swindon, and take them they did, making front page news on four occasions in the *Angling Times*.

Train's Terror—Black
TAIL. Golden pheasant tippets in a fan.
BODY. Silver tinsel ribbed silver wire.
Front Hook
BODY. As rear hook.
HACKLE. Dyed red hen.
WING. Three or four fibres of green peacock sword flanked by two black cock hackles extending to the bend of rear hook.

Train's Terror—Olive
As the black version but olive hackles replacing the black ones.

The Mallard and White Lure (Train)
TAIL. Golden pheasant tippets.
BODY. Silver tinsel ribbed with silver wire.
Front Hook
BODY. As rear hook.
HACKLE. White hen.

WING. Mallard flank feather, white cock hackle either side.
CHEEK. Jungle cock.
HEAD. White.

The Mallard and Yellow (Train)
As the last pattern by using a yellow hackle and yellow hackle flanks and a yellow head.

The Mallard and Blue (Train)
As the other patterns but using a blue hackle, blue hackle flanks and this time a red head.

Train's Badger Lure
TAIL. Golden pheasant tippets.
BODY. Silver tinsel ribbed silver wire.
Front Hook
BODY. As rear hook.
HACKLE. Hot orange hen.
WING. Four badger cock hackles.
CHEEK. Jungle cock.
HEAD. Black.

The Greenwell Lure (Train)
TAIL. None.
BODY. Silver tinsel ribbed silver wire.
Front Hook
BODY. As rear hook.
WING. Four greenwell hackles extending well beyond the
rear hook.

Another lure named after a modern reservoir is the Hanningfield Lure, conceived by Richard Walker, who maintains that the lure is equally good for both brown and rainbow trout. This lure differs from many of the other tandem flies in that the tail is a wound hackle and not the more usual hackle fibre or tag type lure. This perch-type lure is also very effective for adult perch.

The Hanningfield Lure (Walker)

TAIL.   Orange cock hackle wound as an actual hackle.
BODY.   White fluorescent wool ribbed silver tinsel thread.

Front Hook

BODY.   As rear hook.
HACKLE.   Two, the first a short spike hackle bright blue, followed by a hot orange hackle.
WING.   White goat hair topped by strips of speckled turkey.
HEAD.   Black.

The lure that is diametrically opposed to the Black Lure is of course the White Lure. This lure has been particularly effective on such reservoirs as Chew Valley and Blagdon.

The White Lure

TAIL.   White hackle fibres (optional).
BODY.   White wool silver twist ribbing.

Front Hook

BODY.   As rear hook.
HACKLE.   White cock.
WING.   Four white saddle hackles.
CHEEK.   Jungle cock (optional).
HEAD.   Black.

Eric Tavener in his book *Salmon Fishing* (Seeley Service) gives an illustration of the following lure as a tandem double-hook lure. It is also an example of a built-strip wing.

The Norsk Lure

TAIL.   Scarlet Ibis or dyed swan or goose.
BODY.   Oval silver tinsel.

Front Hook

BODY.   As rear hook. (The linkage between the two hooks is also covered).
WING.   Alternating strips of white swan and speckled bustard or turkey, (swan/bustard/swan/bustard).
HACKLE.   Collar style long badger.

Three non-streamer type lures that have evolved from conventional hackled wet flies, and are used with great success on our still waters, are the Worm Fly, the Tandem Black and Peacock Spider and the Tandem Black Pennell.

The Worm Fly

TAIL. Red DFM wool.
BODY. Bronze peacock herl.
HACKLE. Natural red game hen.

Front Hook

TAIL. None.
BODY. Bronze peacock herl.
HACKLE. Natural red game hen.

Tandem Black Pennell

TAIL. Golden pheasant tippet fibres.
BODY. Black floss silk flat silver rib.
HACKLE. Long fibred black hen.

Front Hook

TAIL. None.
BODY. Black floss silk flat silver rib.
HACKLE. Long fibred black hen.

Tandem Black and Peacock

TAIL. None. (I have seen some versions with a small tuft of red DFM floss.)
BODY. Bronze peacock herl.
HACKLE. Black hen.

Front Hook

TAIL. None.
BODY. Bronze peacock herl.
HACKLE. Black hen.

The worm fly is based on the single hook, traditional Red Tag. The tandem Black Pennell is the double version of Cholmondelly Pennell's trout and seatrout fly. The tandem Black and Peacock is derived from the Black and Peacock Spider mentioned very fully in T. C. Ivens well known book *Stillwater Fly Fishing*.

[8]

Minnows and Sticklebacks

The first few patterns tied to represent the minnows or sticklebacks are neither streamers nor bucktail flies, but such flies as the polystickle by its fame and fish-taking properties deserve their place in a book dealing with lures that are basically tied to represent small fish.

A lure that has fished well since its creation by T. C. Ivens, the well known author of *Stillwater Fly Fishing* is the Jersey Herd. Mr. Ivens informs us that this particular fly obtained its name from the foil top off a bottle of Jersey milk. Though other modern dressings have superseded this fly, it still figures highly in the list of fish taking lures and can only be left out of the fly box at one's peril. Since the Jersey Herd came on the scene other hybrids have followed, namely the Silver Herd, the Yellow Herd and, one that I am asked to tie for one angler, a Red Tagged Silver Herd. The dressing of the Jersey Herd utilising Mylar tubing has been given in the chapter on Mylar but another body material I have used which allows the tyer to dispense with an underbody and tie the fly much quicker is 'Goldfingering'.

The Jersey Herd
  TAIL.   Peacock herl about 8 strands tied in at the tail and
      then brought over the body to form the back of the lure.
  BODY.   Flat gold or copper tinsel over a floss silk underbody
      foundation (the original was copper coloured).
  HACKLE.   Short fibred orange cock.
  HEAD.   Bronze peacock herl as back.

The Silver Herd

TAIL.   Bronze peacock herl (as for conventional Jersey Herd).
BODY.   Flat silver tinsel.
HACKLE.   Red (dyed) cock.
HEAD.   Bronze peacock herl.

The Yellow Herd

As for Silver Herd but having a yellow hackle.

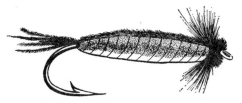

Fig. 21   Jersey Herd

Red Tagged Herd

As for Silver Herd but with the addition of a red wool tail.

All of these flies can be weighted by means of copper or lead wire spiralled beneath the underbody, and are fished with a fairly fast recovery for the best results.

The next group of flies is the well-known polystickle family. There can be very few anglers that have not used or heard of this lure. John Veniard refers to this fly and the Muddler Minnow as two of the flies that truly can be described as being new in design and concept.

As far as the polystickle is concerned it was the case of two anglers with a common theme in mind working quite independently. Richard Walker the well known author and angler, and the well liked and well informed bailiff of Weirwood Reservoir Ken Sinfoil, both designed their lures as fish imitations. In the case of Richard Walker an imitation to represent the prolific stickleback of Grafham Water, and in Ken Sinfoil's case a small fry imitation. Both these imitations came together in Richard Walker's fly vice and the polystickle was born.

Sinfoil's Fry (as tied by Dave Colyer)

This lure is a representation of the very small fry in the earlier stages of its development, at a time when it is almost transparent.

TAIL.   None.

UNDERBODY.   Flat silver tinsel.

OVERBODY.   Polythene strip.

THROAT.   A short tag of red floss silk.

BACK.   Brown mallard feather.

HEAD.   Black with white painted eye (it is noticeable in the young of most fish that the eye is extremely pronounced, therefore there is a case for the optic addition).

As far as polythene is concerned for the tying of the above fly and the following polystickles I have found that a 250 gauge polythene is by far the best gauge to use, as this allows that little stretch which is required in the dressing of such lures.

Stickle Fly (Walker)

TAIL.   Brown turkey or mallard feather cut to a fish tail and tied down. The rest of the feather provides the back of the lure in the same way that the peacock herl does for the Jersey Herd.

BODY.   White floss silver rib.

THROAT.   Red wool.

HEAD.   Black.

Grafham Stickle (Walker)

TAIL AND BACK.   As previous fly.

BODY.   Yellow floss gold rib.

THROAT.   As above fly.

HEAD.   Black.

The first mention of the Stickle flies was made in the November issue of *Trout and Salmon* for 1966. In an article by Richard Walker, he mentions the fact that these flies had accounted at that time for more trout over 5 lbs than any other lure or fly. By January 1967 the use of polythene as a body medium for the Stickle flies had been evolved and yet another article in the pages of *Trout and Salmon* extolled the virtues of this new Stickle—'The Polystickle'. In this article by Richard Walker he credits Ken Sinfoil with the innovation of polythene as a body medium, and at this time too the artificial raffia 'Raffene' came into existence as the back and tail

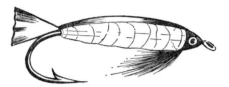

Fig. 22   Polystickle

of the fly. The use of nickel-plated hooks aids the tier in so much that the silver underbody can be dispensed with and the polythene can be wound directly on to the bare hook, bare that is except for a wide spiralling of tying silk to simulate the ribs of the small fish. The Raffene must be dampened and stretched before tying in.

The following four polystickles are all based on the original lures as tied by Richard Walker, and are the ones that I personally am asked to tie and have given me most success fish-wise. The strange thing about this type of lure is that a great number of fish are taken when it is slowly dragged nymphwise along the bottom as when fished fast at other depths. Further stickle-type flies are given in the chapter on additional patterns.

Black Polystickle

TAIL AND BACK.   Black Raffene.

BODY.   250 gauge polythene wound on over a nickel hook, a winding of red floss is wound at the rear of the head to simulate the innards of the fry.

HACKLE.   A short dyed red beard hackle.

HEAD.   Black.

Brown Polystickle

TAIL AND BACK.   Brown Raffene.

BODY.   As previous fly.
HACKLE.   Dyed orange.
HEAD.   Black.

Green Polystickle

TAIL AND BACK.   Dark green Raffene.
BODY.   As previous flies.
HACKLE.   Fibres of bronze mallard flank.
HEAD.   Black.

White Polystickle

TAIL AND BACK.   White Raffene.
BODY.   As previous flies with the addition of a white fluores-
cent wool underbody.
HACKLE.   White cock.
HEAD.   Black.

All of these flies can have an additional external ribbing of black
tying silk over the polythene, and the further addition of a white
painted eye with a black pupil enhances the appearance of the fly
if it does nothing else.

Colonel Jocelyn Lane in his interesting and informative book
Lake and Loch Fishing (Seeley Service), gives a dressing for a stickleback representation which he found successful at such times as
the trout were seeking the same.

Stickleback (Lane)

SILK.   Golden Olive.
TAIL.   Two olive cock hackles back to back and cut to a fishtail shape.
BODY.   Underbody of pale straw coloured silk, close coils of
silver thread over.
BACK.   Olive cock hackle fibres the length of the hook tied in
at the head and bound down with wide turns of tying silk
to halfway along the shank, the tips are then cut off and
all loose fibres trimmed off, but some are left untrimmed
to represent the spiny dorsal fin.
HACKLE.   Dyed red beard hackle.

In August 1967 there appeared in the pages of *Trout and Salmon* an article by Conrad Voss Bark, this was considered one of the best fishing articles of that year and was subsequently republished in the *Angler's Annual*. This article dealt with a fly as used by the author's grandfather, to represent a minnow, and was used with great success at Blagdon earlier this century. The dressing Conrad Voss Bark gives for his grandfather's fly was as follows:

Blagdon Minnow

TAIL AND BACK. Rolled brown mallard.
BODY. Either silver or gold.
HACKLE. Palmered off white, or orange.
THROAT. Orange or red beard hackle.

The body of this fly is built up in much the same way as Lane's stickleback in order to obtain a fishlike shape.

A pattern of the streamer type that I evolved and found successful for both brown and rainbow trout is the Minnow Streamer. I tied both a male and female pattern just in case the trout I was seeking had a particular preference to either sex, or had misogynistic tendencies. Incidentally they did not appear to have, and both patterns killed equally well.

Minnow Streamer

Male

TAIL. Blue dun hackle fibres.
BODY. White floss or wool silver rib.
HACKLE. Dyed red beard hackle.
WING. Dark olive cock hackles back to back, strips of barred teal or mallard either side.
CHEEK. Jungle cock tied short.
HEAD. Olive green top, white lacquer underneath.

Minnow Streamer

Female

Exactly the same as the male dressing, but with a blue dun hackle replacing the dyed red.

With the scarcity of jungle cock the cheeks can be dispensed with and a black and white eye painted on the head of the fly instead.

The following pattern of mine when dry looks like a sparse grotesque motheaten shaving brush but it takes on a very minnow like appearance in the water. The secret in dressing this fly is not to overdress, a habit we all fall into when we first dress hairwing flies. One evening whilst fishing with this particular fly, and slowly despairing of catching a trout for supper, I had a thumping take. could almost taste the succulent red flesh of a large browny. Then it slowly dawned on me that the fish was performing a little erratically for either a brown or rainbow trout. Well, when the fish came to the net it turned out to be a fighting two pound roach, a lovely sight, all silver and red with my fly firmly hooked in the top lip. I slid him or her gratefully back into the water, for it was the only fish I caught that evening. I did not have a fresh trout supper, but I had caught the most beautiful roach I had seen for a long time.

Since the dressing for this fly, The Hairy Bucktail, was published in John Veniard's book *Reservoir and Lake Flies*, other anglers have had success with this fly, one in particular taking six trout at Chew and Blagdon, the best being a Brown of $3\frac{1}{2}$ lbs and a rainbow of 3 lbs and the smallest just over 2 lbs. Not a bad catch on a motheaten shaving brush!

The Hairy Bucktail Minnow

TAIL.   A short tuft of red wool.

BODY.   Flat silver tinsel silver rib.

OVERWING.   White bucktail, green bucktail over.

UNDERWING.   White bucktail to bend of the hook, and a short spike hackle of red cock.

HEAD.   Black white eye, black pupil.

A. C. R. Howman (Alastair Ross) in John Veniard's book gives his dressing for the stickleback which is very similar in design to Colonel Jocelyn Lane's stickleback fly.

British Streamers and Bucktails

FIRST ROW. DEVISED AND TIED BY DAVID TRAIN
Black Hairwing   Fluorescent Badger Hairwing   Pheasant Darta   Red & White Lure

SECOND ROW. DEVISED BY R. A. STEPHENS OF STEVENAGE, HERTS
Mylar Texas Rose   Mylar Olive   Mylar Black

THIRD ROW. DEVISED BY R. A. STEPHENS
John Thomas   Ashanti   Featherwing

FOURTH ROW
Black & Orange Marabou (*Price*)   Adbry Streamer (*Bradbury*)   Black Marabou (*Price*)

FIFTH ROW
Tadpole Streamer (*Price*)   Banded Squirrel Bucktail (*Price*)   Orange Bodied
Muddler (*Iveson*)   Green Perch fry (*Price*)

SIXTH ROW
Golden Anna (*Price*)   Blue Flash (*Price*)   Orange Streamer (*Price*)

SEVENTH ROW. DEVISED AND TIED BY DAVID SHEWAN OF ABERDEEN
Black Silver cheek   Silver Nylon   Grey Silver cheek

EIGHTH ROW. SUPPLIED BY MESSRS FARLOWS OF PALL MALL
Black Murderer   Red AA Lure   Silver Murderer

Stickleback (Howman)
> TAIL.   Wide olive hackle cut to shape.
> UNDERBODY.   Copperwire and white floss.
> OVERBODY.   Flat silver tinsel.
> BACK.   Olive cock trimmed to shape to give a dorsal fin.
> THROAT.   Mixed olive and red hackle.

A. Courteney Williams in his famous book *A Dictionary of Trout Flies*, a book which is to my mind the fly tyer's bible and deserves to be read by all fly fishermen for sheer interest's sake, gives four patterns which can be described as minnow representations. These flies, which Mr. Williams attributes to Captain J. J. Dunne for fishing at Blagdon, are more or less of streamer conception. Mr. Williams further informs us that these flies were particularly effective in New Zealand, and goes on to say that prodigious catches were made with them.

The first two are the Reckless William and Reckless William's Mate, both tied as streamer flies on longshank hooks, having long strips of mobile feather for wings. With the wealth of minnow type streamers and polystickles etc. that are now at our disposal, flies such as the Reckless William are sadly out of fashion, but I for one feel it worth while resurrecting such flies, for they took good fish once and can do so again.

The Reckless William (Dunne/Courteney Williams)
> TAG.   Four turns gold wire.
> BODY.   One third flat silver followed by four turns of flat gold tinsel, then white floss.
> HACKLE.   Orange.
> WING.   Pheasant tail dyed olive either side of the hook and a strip of green swan over the back.
> HEAD.   Green.

Reckless William's Mate (Dunne/Courteney Williams)
> TAG.   Four turns of oval gold tinsel.
> TAIL.   Golden pheasant crest.
> BODY.   As for Reckless William.

F

HACKLE.   Orange.

WING.   Silver Amherst pheasant tail dyed light olive, strip of yellow swan under.

The next two of Captain J. J. Dunne's flies have indeed been revived in lure form, or more precisely in the multi hook type of lure. These flies are called the Missionary and, to avoid confusion, The Orange Missionary. The original dressing given by Courteney Williams gave a conventional hook rather than a longshank, but he did intimate that the wing should extend well beyond the bend. I have tied both Missionaries on long shank hooks streamer style and have had success with both brown and rainbow trout. They can be quite a soul-saving fly for those blank days.

Missionary

TAIL.   White cock hackle fibres.

BODY.   Spun white wool (silver rib optional).

HACKLE.   White cock.

WING.   Black turkey or dyed black swan, flanked either side with barred teal.

Orange Missionary

As for conventional Missionary but with an orange hackle and tail.

The fly tying firm of Tom Saville Ltd. supply this fly as a tandem lure.

Three American patterns that I have used with some degree of success for both species of trout are The Alaska Mary, The Blacknose Dace and the Cut Lips. These flies tied with species of small fish in the U.S.A. in mind, take our home bred trout with no distinction. They are very fortunate in America having a very varied small fish population with which to make copies and lures. Colonel Joseph Bates Jnr. in his book *Streamer Fly Tying and Fishing*, Edson Leonard in his book *Flies*, and John Veniard in his two books *A Further Guide to Fly Dressing*, and *Reservoir and Lake Flies*, give many examples of these transatlantic fish imitations that are worth giving a try on our own waters.

However the best flies are the ones you tie yourself from your own observations of small fish. A fly of your own creation that catches fish becomes more than a flutter of feathers or a bunch of hair, it becomes the very extension of yourself, a small portion of your personality attached to your cast. Catch fish with it and the feeling of satisfaction is surely hard to beat, nothing can really compare with it. Try it!

Alaska Mary
TAIL. Red hackle fibres or red floss or wool.
BODY. White wool or chenille silver rib.
WING. White polar bear or bucktail.
CHEEK. Jungle cock.

Blacknose Dace (as tied by Keel Fly Co.)
TAIL. Red wool.
BODY. Flat silver tinsel.
WING. White bucktail, black bucktail over, brown bucktail-over that.
HACKLE. None on keel hook version, white bucktail on conventional hook.

Cut Lips
TAIL. Blue dun hackle fibres.
BODY. Light mauve wool silver rib.
WING. Olive saddle hackles.
HACKLE. Blue dun.

[9]

Other Fish Imitations

It is a known fact that large fish can and do eat small fish, and it is in the main the large wily old fish that become ninety per cent piscivorous. The small fish they eat are the indigenous species of the area. In most waters the perch fry figures highly in the diet of the larger trout. This is certainly true of natural lakes and, in many cases, our newer reservoirs. In other waters, because they are there, roach and rudd fry are taken by both rainbow and brown trout. All these small coarse fish soon establish themselves in the reservoirs, and at the time of writing Grafham water is being inundated with large quantities of perch, and only regular netting and trapping can keep down their numbers.

The majestic and rare trout of the river Thames for years have been sought with a metallic lure or by spinning or livebaiting with the little bleak. There is no finer bait for these large trout than the bleak, but to my knowledge nobody appears to fish for these

Fig. 23   Perch Fry Streamer

large predators with a streamer lure tied to represent this little fish whose scales in the past gave the glitter to artificial pearls long before the days of culture and cultured pearls. It is a fact that these

Thames trout are few and far between but a good imitator pattern fished correctly in the right places stands as good a chance of paying off as any other type of artificial lure.

The following list of dressings is intended to represent the coarse fish of this country that can be taken as part of the large trout's diet. They include lures tied to represent the fry of the roach, the rudd, and the fry of those little green barred tigers, the perch. In an earlier chapter, dressings for the bullhead and loach were given tied in the 'Muddler's' style, these can also be simulated by other dressings.

The infant brown and rainbow trout often provide a *cordon bleu* meal for the adult fish. An empty belly and easy prey causes the trout to have no scruples in this direction. And even the tiny salmon parr falls victim to larger trout and seatrout. What of the pike? The number of small jack pike that are caught by anglers only to be engulfed in a huge maw of a bigger pike are too numerous to count.

Perch Streamer (Price)
TAIL.   Orange cock hackles.

BODY.   Gold mylar marked with dark vertical lines with a felt tip pen.

WING.   Two grizzles hackles dyed a yellowish green, two light grey hackles either side.

UNDERBODY.   Two white cock hackles as long as the wing.

HACKLE.   (Throat) Orange cock.

SHOULDER.   Hen pheasant body feather (dark centre light buff outer).

CHEEK.   Jungle cock.

Roach Streamer (Price)
TAIL.   Dyed red cock hackles with an equal quantity of olive above.

BODY.   White wool, flat silver rib.

WING.   Two white cock hackles flanked by two dark olive hackles.

UNDERBODY.   Two white cock hackles as long as the wing.

HACKLE.   (Throat) Dyed red cock hackle.
SHOULDER.   Lady Amhurst tippet either side of the wing.
CHEEK.   Jungle cock.

Hair Wing Roach Fry (Train)

TAIL.   A fan of grey mallard body feathers.
BODY.   White wool covered with wide silver tinsel and ribbed oval tinsel.
WING.   Strands of blue bucktail, white over this and black squirrel over the white.
HACKLE.   (Throat) White hen.
CHEEK.   Jungle cock.
HEAD.   White.

Perch Fry Silver (Saville)

TAIL.   Golden pheasant tippets in a fan.
BODY.   Embossed silver tinsel.
HACKLE.   Red hackle fibres.
WING.   Two olive hackles flanked by two cree hackles.
CHEEK.   Jungle cock.

There is a gold version of this fly also tied by Savilles of Beeston which only varies from the above pattern in that the body is of embossed gold and not silver tinsel.

Roach Fry Lure (Saville)

TAIL.   Dyed red hackle fibres.
BODY.   Embossed silver tinsel.
HACKLE.   Blue dun.
WING.   Four medium olive cock hackles.
CHEEK.   Jungle cock.

Perch Fry (Downs)

TAIL.   Cream hackle fibres.
BODY.   White floss silk covered with polythene as for poly-stickle.
HACKLE.   A beard of scarlet hen hackle fibres.

WING. Two natural red hen hackles barred with a felt-tip pen.

This last fly was devised by Donald Downs who not only is a competent fly dresser and angler, but is better known as the illustrator of John Veniard's books and Geoffrey Bucknall's. His work also appears each month in the pages of *Trout and Salmon* magazine.

Green Perch Fry (Price)
TAIL. Orange cock hackle fibres.
BODY. Green lurex gold oval rib.
HACKLE. Orange cock.
WING. Olive dyed squirrel tail.
CHEEK. Jungle cock.

There is a small anecdote attached to the last fly which, incidentally, I tied as a weedless version. One Saturday morning a chap came into the shop asking for some spinners. 'What for?' I asked. 'Trout' came back the swift reply. 'You don't want spinners for trout. Why don't you try a fly or lure, it's far more satisfying to catch a trout on a fly you know' I replied pedantically.

Well the upshot was that this person who shall remain anonymous purchased the above lure. A week or two later, via another person, I was informed that the chap to whom I sold the Perch Bucktail had four good size trout on the lure. The pleasure at the news was soon nullified when I discovered that the trout were poached from our club's lake. Well, you can't win them all. But he did use a fly!

Bleak Streamer (Price)
TAIL. Mixed blue dun and light olive hackle.
BODY. White wool silver rib.
HACKLE. Mixed as for tail.
WING. Four white cock hackles.
CHEEK. Silver mylar strip.
HEAD. Olive white eye black pupil.

Loach Streamer (Price)

    TAIL.   Olive cock hackle fibres.

    BODY.   Mixed buff coloured fur and hare's ear, rib oval gold
    or silver tinsel.

    HACKLE.   Olive throat, two white hackles as underbody.

    WING.   Four cree hackles, the darker the better.

    SHOULDER.   Hen pheasant body feathers.

    CHEEK.   Jungle cock tied short.

Fig. 24   Roach Fry Streamer

The silvery dace of our streams and crystal rivers can be
imitated by that very mobile feather the marabou. A marabou
fly fished in the fast water can prove very attractive to predatory
fish. As it is recovered the pulsating feathers simulate that natural
fish wriggle which fish such as pike find irresistible.

Marabou Dace

    TAIL.   None.

    BODY.   Flat silver ribbed oval silver, or silver Mylar tubing.

    HACKLE.   Mixed light olive and red.

    WING.   White marabou with green marabou over.

The following patterns are intended to represent the babies of
the game fish world. The first called the Brown Trout Streamer
does not look much like a natural brown trout on the face of it,
but in the water it appears very lifelike, having a natural coloration.

Brown Trout Streamer

    TAIL.   A tuft of olive green hackle fibres.

    BODY.   Thin tapered fish like green floss.

RIB. Flat gold tinsel.

HACKLE. Underbody of long white cock with a beard hackle of olive green.

WING. Six cock hackles, two brown hackles back to back, two olive hackles either side, two badger hackles on the outside of these.

CHEEK. Jungle cock.

Pink Rainbow Streamer

TAIL. Olive green hackle fibres.

BODY. White wool silver rib.

WING. Four pink hackles, green peacock herl over.

UNDER WING. Two white cock hackles, a beard or spike of green hackle fibres between.

CHEEK. Jungle cock.

John Veniard in his book *Reservoir and Lake Flies* gives amongst his American patterns the following flies:

Little Brown Trout

TAIL. Cream hackle fibres.

BODY. Pale yellow wool.

WING. Yellow marabou, red marabou over, beige hen hackle fibres over.

SIDES. Strips of gold mylar.

HEAD. Black yellow eyes with black pupil.

Brook Trout

TAIL. None.

BODY. Rear two thirds white floss, remainder pink floss.

RIB. Medium gold tinsel.

THROAT. Orange hackle fibres then black fibres then white fibres.

WING. Hot orange bucktail, yellow dyed grizzle over this, followed by olive green hackles.

CHEEK. Jungle cock.

HEAD. Black.

Another Rainbow imitation used the Goldfingering material mentioned earlier.

Rainbow Bucktail

TAIL.   Olive hackle fibres.

BODY.   Pink Goldfingering Ref. WG7.

WING.   White bucktail, green bucktail over.

UNDER WING.   White bucktail, spike of olive hackle fibres.

CHEEK.   Jungle cock (a painted eye can be substituted for this feather).

HEAD.   Olive green top, white below.

[10]

The Attractors

It is probably true to say that this group of bizarre and beautiful flies has caught more anglers than fish. It is also true to say that this kind of fly has a place in our lure box if only to use when all other flies and lures have failed.

I believe that this type of lure prompts the trout to rise in what I have described earlier as 'an anger take'. The flies are also useful early in the season to stir the lethargic trout from their winter

Fig. 25 Matuka

torpor. A flasher fly, an abstract of fur and bright feather, nine times out of ten will do the trick. It is not a hard and fast rule but in fishing there can be no hard or fast rules.

The traditional salmon patterns used for many years on our rivers can be classed as attractors, for there appears to be no counterpart in nature either swimming, floating or flying that resembles most of these beautiful creations we term flies. But what these flies do is to cause the salmon to take notice and strike and often be caught. So it is with the gaudy streamer lures and that is why I will never be without one or two patterns in different sizes to fall back on when the most exquisitely contrived imitation has failed to move a single fish.

On those frustrating occasions when the trout are preoccupied with a particular item of food and are being particularly selective in their feeding, a streamer pattern flopped almost carelessly on the water can often take a fish that on stomach examination reveals a gorging on a particular nymph or fly. I have taken fish chock-full of nymphs on a fly such as a large Marabou Muddler.

Though we make a definite distinction between these groups of flies and the fish imitators they do at least have one similarity—an aquatic shape. Practically all the flasher flies have the fish-like shape which in itself can prove attractive to the trout.

It is often difficult to come to a decision as to what is a flasher or attractor lure, or what is a representative pattern. The patterns listed in this chapter are my own choice.

I have always found that rainbow trout are attracted to the colour orange. The following streamer is just one of many using orange as its main coloration.

Orange Streamer (Price)

TAIL.   None.
BODY.   Orange floss gold oval rib.
HACKLE.   None.
WING.   Two orange hackles, two grey badger outside.
CHEEK.   Jungle cock.

One of the famous trout flies of the flasher variety is the Alexandra. Like many flasher flies it is reputed to represent a small fish. I suppose it could be so, but as far as the streamer version is concerned I prefer to include it with the attractor patterns rather than in the preceding chapter on more direct representational flies. In its time, and in its conventional, streamer, and multi-hook versions, this fly has accounted for many fish and its popularity in this modern age hasn't lessened.

Alexandra Streamer (Popular in Canada)

TAIL.   Red Ibis and a few strands of green peacock herl.
BODY.   Silver flat tinsel ribbed oval silver.

HACKLE. Black hen.
WING. Strands of matching green peacock sword herl.
CHEEK. Strips of red ibis.

A lure that is extremely popular in the U.S.A. that has evolved from a standard British trout fly is the Royal Coachman Bucktail. It is quite remarkable how a fly originally tied with some sort of moth in mind has evolved many miles away as a streamer fly.

Royal Coachman Bucktail (U.S.A.)

TAIL. Golden pheasant tippets.
BODY. In three parts green herl, then red floss, then green herl again.
HACKLE. Brown.
WING. White bucktail.
CHEEK. Jungle cock tied short.

Other variations of this fly are given in the chapter on additional patterns.

A fly that has appeared in most books dealing with streamer lures is the Chief Needahbeh, named after a real Red Indian chief of the Penobscot Indians of Main. I must admit it has never caught a fish for me. It has for others, but never for me, but I include it because it was the first streamer pattern I ever tied and it looks so attractive to boot.

Chief Needahbeh (U.S.A.)

TAIL. None.
TAG. Three turns of silver tinsel.
BODY. Scarlet floss oval silver rib.
WING. Two yellow hackles, two orange outside.
HACKLE. Mixed yellow and scarlet.
CHEEK. Jungle cock.

Two attractive flies I have had success with are the Golden Anna and Silver Anna. I needed some new flasher flies for early season fishing so I tied these two flies with this in mind and both caught trout. The golden version was also quite successful for jack pike, taking them up to 6 lbs. The dressings are as follows:

The Golden Anna (Price)
TAIL. Yellow swan.
BODY. Embossed gold tinsel.
HACKLE. Lemon yellow.
WING. Two lemon yellow hackles, two badger either side.
CHEEK. Jungle cock.

The Silver Anna (Price)
TAIL. Red swan.
BODY. Embossed silver tinsel.
HACKLE. Scarlet cock.
WING. Two lemon yellow hackles, two cree hackles either side.
CHEEK. Jungle cock.

The following spectral flies have proved very popular with both trout and seatrout anglers all over the world, the Grey Ghost also being effective for both the Atlantic and Pacific salmon. The following three flies are American in origin.

Black Ghost (U.S.A.)
TAIL. Golden pheasant crest.
BODY. Black wool silver rib.
HACKLE. Golden pheasant crest or yellow hackle.
WING. Four white hackles.
CHEEK. Jungle cock.

Grey Ghost (U.S.A.)
TAIL. None.
BODY. Orange wool or floss silk.
HACKLE. Strands of bronze peacock herl, then white bucktail, finally yellow hackle fibres.
WING. Four blue dun hackle fibres.
CHEEK. Lady Amhurst tippet feathers (original dressing calls for silver argus pheasant, but this is difficult to obtain).

Brown Ghost (U.S.A.)

    TAIL. None.

    TAG. Silver tinsel.

    BODY. Brown floss silk silver tinsel rib.

    HACKLE. Few strands of bronze peacock herl, then a few strands white bucktail, finally a golden pheasant crest pointing upward.

    WING. Golden pheasant crest feather, four brown hackles over.

    SHOULDER. Teal body feather dyed brown.

    CHEEK. Jungle cock.

Of all the lures in use today whether of the single or tandem hook variety the Black Lure family is to my mind by far and away

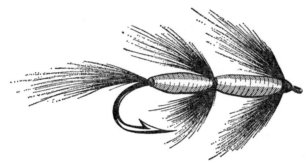

Fig. 26 Fuzzy Wuzzy

the most popular. One fly that has been successful for reservoir trout early in the season or any time at dusk is the Painted Lady. This is no more than a tarted up version of the Black Lure tied with odd scraps of feather left on my fly bench after I had been tying some salmon flies.

Painted Lady (Price)

    TAIL. Blue guinea fowl.

    BODY. Black floss thinly dressed flat silver rib.

    HACKLE. Magenta.

    WING. Black cock hackles.

    CHEEK. Jungle cock.

Another Black Lure that I tie for one particular client is the Lady Midnight, this client has a preference for a complete black fly with no adornments or flash.

Lady Midnight (Price)
>   TAIL.   Black hackle fibres.
>   BODY.   Black chenille.
>   HACKLE.   Black collar.
>   WING.   Black cock hackles.

Fig. 27   Painted Lady Streamer

One of the more popular dark flies of recent years was devised by Richard Walker. There are not many fly companies that do not have the Sweeny Todd on their lists.

Sweeny Todd (Walker)
>   TAIL.   None.
>   BODY.   Black silk silver rib fine oval.
>   HACKLE.   Magenta.
>   WING.   Black squirrel fibres.
>   BENEATH THE WING.   Some fluorescent magenta silk is tied in.

Mention has been made of marabou as a winging medium for streamer lures. This fluffy feather provides the winging medium for many modern flies. The following simple black lure is extremely effective on our reservoirs early in the season.

Black Marabou (Price)
>   TAIL.   None.
>   BODY.   Black chenille flat silver rib.
>   WING.   Black marabou.

The following marabou fly has proved successful for me time and time again. It is just a variation of the above fly, but I prefer this one:

Black and Orange Marabou (Price)
TAIL. Orange hackle fibres.
BODY. Flat gold tinsel.
HACKLE. Orange beard hackle.
WING. Black marabou.
CHEEK. Jungle cock.

New Zealand has long been famous for the size of its rainbow and brown trout population, especially in lake Rotaru and the more famous lake Taupo. The rainbow was introduced successfully in about 1883, the brown trout a little earlier. Up until this time the waterways of New Zealand were virtually devoid of any large fish, there was an absence of sporting game fish and the rivers held only small species of no consequence to the angler.

After the trouts' introduction to these waters they thrived and grew to prodigious sizes on the lush new aqueous pastures, a ten-pounder being a small fish. To catch these monster trout the New Zealanders evolved new styles of lures and flies. These lures are included here because of their unique methods of winging. John Veniard, in his book *Lake and Reservoir Flies*, gives full instructions and many dressings of such flies, so I only include a few in this book, however the combination of dressings are limitless as one can appreciate.

In Matuka dressings it will be seen that the wing is tied down along the body of the lure by means of the ribbing medium. In the whole feather wing a series of game body feathers are tied to flank the body of the fly.

The royal title 'Imperial' is given to any Matuka winged fly that is adorned with a jungle cock cheek. Do not be afraid to use these strange flies on British waters, they can be killers for in the water they have an attractive undulating mobility that trout find irresistible.

G

Black Imperial Matuka
  TAIL. None.
  BODY. Black chenille.
  RIB. Flat silver tinsel.
  WING. Four black hackles.
  HACKLE. None.

Green Matuka
  TAIL. None.
  BODY. Green chenille.
  RIB. Gold tinsel.
  WING. Four brown cock hackles or furnace.
  HACKLE. None.

The above flies are based on original New Zealand patterns, further examples are given in the chapter on additional streamer patterns.

The other style of winging prevalent in New Zealand is the whole feather type of lure, an example is given below. This fly was presumably named after the present Duchess of Windsor before her marriage to Edward VIII the now present Duke.

Mrs. Simpson
  TAIL. Black squirrel fibres.
  BODY. Chenille colour unimportant.
  WING. A minimum of four pairs of brown partridge, the smallest pair at the tail end tied in first, the others tied in consecutively overlapping along.

This fly is sometimes called 'Killer Style'.

So far from New Zealand we have mentioned the 'Matuka Winging' and the Killer type of fly. There are basically four other types of fly peculiar to New Zealand—the Fuzzy series, Split Wing, Pukeko, and Furskin series.

Fuzzy Wuzzy
  TAIL. Black squirrel fibres.

BODY. (In three or four parts depending on the size of hook) Red chenille.

HACKLES. (Separating each body portion). Black hackle, largest at the head.

Fig. 28   Whole Feather

The split-wing type is similar to the Matuka style without the tying down and using split game bird feathers.

Yellow Partridge
TAIL.   Yellow hackle fibres.
BODY.   Yellow chenille.
RIB.   Oval silver tinsel.
WING.   Split partridge tail.
HACKLE.   Natural red.

The Pukeko like the Matuka flies are named after respective New Zealand birds from which the original flies were named. Small dyed heron feathers are a good substitute for Pukeko feathers.

Pukeko and Red
TAIL.   Red wool.
BODY.   Red chenille.
WING.   Three blue pukeko feathers (dyed heron).
HACKLE.   Red cock.

The fur skin type of fly is represented by the New Zealand fly, The Rabbit.

The Rabbit (Red)

TAIL. Red cock hackle fibres.

BODY. Red chenille.

WING. (Thin strip of rabbit) extending beyond the bend of the hook.

RIB. Oval silver tinsel tying down the skin matuka style.

HACKLE. None.

In the book *A Further Guide to Fly Dressing*, John Veniard also includes streamer patterns from South Africa. It is interesting to note that South African flies have greater affinity with the New Zealand flies, whilst the flies of Australia are of the more conventional style and size.

Amongst the many South African flies that Mr. Veniard gives is the Walkers Black Widow.

Walkers Black Widow

TAIL. None.

BODY. Red Floss

RIB. Oval silver tinsel.

WINGS. Black hackles tied down matuka style.

CHEEK. Jungle cock.

Apart from this style of fly South Africa also makes use of the whole feather or 'Killer' patterns.

As can be easily appreciated, the lures used in Canada are in the main the same streamers and bucktails used by their American cousins. However, the Canadians have a preference for the whole feather type of streamer such as the Ashdown Green, The Mickey Finn, Blue Damsel. Another famous fly of the whole wing type is the Coachman Streamer.

Ashdown Green

TAIL. Scarlet duck or goose.

BODY. Claret wool flat gold rib.

WING. White goose wing.

HACKLE. Claret cock.

Mickey Fin
>TAIL. None.
>BODY. Flat silver tinsel.
>RIB. Oval tinsel.
>WING. A built wing of yellow, red, and yellow goose or swan. The uppermost band of yellow is twice the width of the other band.

Blue Damsel
>TAIL. Golden pheasant tippets.
>BODY. Bronze peacock herl.
>WING. Medium blue goose wing quill.
>HACKLE. Collar of blue cock.

[11]

Streamers and Bucktails as Dry Flies

It is always wrongly assumed that streamer and bucktail lures are
inevitably wet flies tied principally to imitate fish or fry. This is
not so as will be seen in this and following chapters.

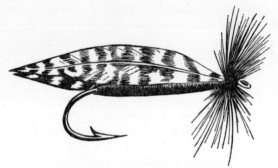

Fig. 29   Stonefly Streamer

All of us at some time or another have witnessed the struggles
of a sick or wounded fish. Floating with very little movement,
belly up on the surface, it is carried by the natural movement of
the lake or by the river current. Occasionally it summons up a
reserve of strength to flick its tail and struggle momentarily
beneath the surface in an endeavour to return completely to its
natural environment. Such fish fall easy prey to the predators such
as trout and pike. Lures that simulate a wounded, sick or stunned
fish can be fished on the surface giving a dry fly dimension to
streamer fishing. Flies that incorporate clipped deer hair or polyurethane foam as body mediums are best suited for this type of

lure. I prefer streamer winging rather than bucktail for this floating lure as the type of movement offered by the feathers lends itself to the wounded fish simulation far better than a hairwing.

Careful observation of wounded fish at the waterside will allow you to provide your streamer with a natural movement, and unlike sunk lures you can of course observe the motivation of your streamer as you manipulate your rod or line.

A method of fishing that I find successful is to allow the fly to float with the natural water movement, then to give the line a twitch, enough to momentarily sink the fly in a flutter of feather, allowing it to resurface and proceed with no line recovery, and then again twitching it below the surface. And so forth.

On the occasions when the trout or pike are making inroads into the small fish of the water it is a good idea to use this method as opposed to the sunk fly. More enjoyment is achieved in seeing your lure savaged by the fish hungry predator as he mops up the stunned minnows etc.

With regard to pattern, any of the standard minnow or fish fry imitations can be used with the addition of either an underbody of balsa wood, cork, polyurethane foam or a clipped deer hair body instead of the more usual body dressing. These lures can also be utilised as buoyant lures with a sinking line, more of this later in the book.

Apart from the fish-type lure there are many large lure-type flies that are tied with other creatures in mind and are fished on the surface as dry flies. I refer to such creatures as grass-hoppers, crickets, stoneflies, etc, that are imitated by streamers and bucktails. As mentioned in the earlier chapter on the Muddler Minnow, this fly is successfully fished on the surface as an imitation, presumably, of the insects so mentioned above. For further imitations we have to resort to established patterns from the U.S.A. as most flies tied in this country to represent the grasshoppers etc. are usually of a conventional rather than a streamer or bucktail conception.

Amongst the American patterns given below are some that were kindly sent to me by the Orvis Company of America. All are basically of streamer and bucktail design.

Letort Cricket

TAIL.   None.

BODY.   Black floss silk.

WING.   Black swan or goose.

HACKLE.   In the form of a collar, long fibres of black bear or squirrel clipped at the head to form a head of the muddler type.

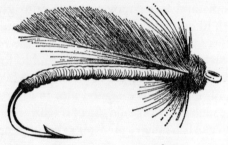

Fig. 30   Letort Cricket

Letort Hopper

TAIL.   None.

BODY.   Yellow floss.

WING.   Oak turkey.

HACKLE.   Unclipped deer hair.

HEAD.   Clipped deer hair (Muddler style).

Bird's Stone Fly

TAIL.   Two or three fine bristles.

BODY.   Orange floss divided into four parts, each part separated by a clipped hair hackle clipped to about $\frac{1}{8}$ inch.

WING.   Brown bucktail or squirrel.

HACKLE.   Clipped squirrel or bucktail (not the soft body hair but the stiffish hair of the tail).

HEAD.   Orange floss, two fine bristle antennae.

The shaggier the better for the above fly.

Deer Hopper

TAIL.   Red swan or goose.

BODY. Yellow dyed clipped deer hair, clipped smooth and cylindrical like an insect's abdomen, except for tail end top surface which is not slipped as much and is left sticking up like a 'cocked up' tail.

WING. Cinnamon turkey clipped short and flanking the body.

HACKLE. Two natural brown cock and grizzle tied collar fashion.

Rio Grande King

TAIL. Golden pheasant tippet.
BODY. Peacock herl.
WING. White bucktail.
HACKLE. Natural red game cock (collar).

A very similar American west coast fly to the Rio Grande King is the Trude.

Trude

TAIL. Red swan or goose strip.
BODY. Peacock herl.
WING. Wing calf tail or bucktail.
HACKLE. Natural red cock (collar).

Cooper's Hopper

TAIL. Red.
BODY. Pale yellow/brown wool, floss or chenille.
HACKLE. Body palmered in olive green cock.
WING. Red squirrel flanked by oak turkey.
HACKLE. Collar, natural red cock.

Like the Trude and Caddis buck lures the Sofa Pillow is an extremely popular fly for both rainbow and cutthroat trout for the American west coast.

Green Sofa Pillow

TAIL. Red swan or goose.
BODY. Green floss ribbed flat silver tinsel.

WING.   Grey squirrel.
HACKLE.   Red game cock.

Red Sofa Pillow
As above but with red floss body.

Yellow Sofa Pillow
As Green Sofa Pillow but with yellow floss body.

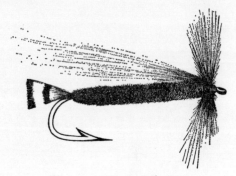

Fig. 31   Rio Grande King

Caddis Buck
TAIL.   None.
BODY.   Deep orange seals fur.
HACKLE.   Palmered furnace cock.
WING.   Brown natural deer hair.

Light Caddis Buck
TAIL.   None.
BODY.   Pale yellow seals fur.
HACKLE.   Palmered blue dun.
WING.   Natural brown deer hair.

Sometimes these last two patterns are given the same coloured tails as the hackles, and on occasions they are referred to as Buck Caddis.

Little Caddis
TAIL.   None.

BODY.   Either orange, yellow or green floss.
HACKLE.   None.
WING.   Above and below the hook spun natural deer body hair.

Another dressing which is only a slight variation of the Caddis Buck is the Dry Bucktail.

Dry Bucktail
TAIL.   Natural light red cock fibres.
BODY.   Orange floss.
HACKLE.   Palmered natural red game cock.
WING.   Brown bucktail.

The difference between the dressings given for these dry flies and such better known American patterns of the 'Hairwing' variety such as the Wulff series is basically in the winging. The Wulff series of flies do not have the long swept back wings of the above patterns but usually have upright wings and heavy hair tails, so by no stretch of the imagination can we really call them bucktails or streamers.

It is also interesting to see that in Courteney Williams' book *A Dictionary of Trout Flies* an illustration appears in the colour plates of a Stone Fly for which there is no accompanying dressing. A note on the colour plate explains that the pattern is a special. This pattern is tied on a long shank hook and has long streamer-type wings.

All these patterns are worth giving a try on those occasions when grasshoppers or stoneflies etc. are abroad; for, let's face it, the good old Muddler fished dry has opened the door already.

Stonefly Streamer
TAIL.   None.
BODY.   Mixed grey and yellow seal fur. Rib gold oval tinsel.
WING.   Grey mottled turkey extending well beyond the hook.
HACKLE.   Natural red game tied as collar.

This dressing is an ideal pattern to represent the larger species of stonefly found on some waters.

[12]

Bucktails as Nymphs and Other Larvae

It has been noted that, quite often, streamers, bucktails and other fish-simulating lures often take fish when the flies are recovered very slowly, or even lying static on the bottom. It is highly probable that the fish mistake such lures for some form of larva or large nymph.

The following group of flies are designed to represent the larger of the aquatic larvae. These flies differ from the more conventional

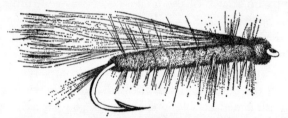

Fig. 32   Picket Pin

nymph patterns in so much as they utilise longshank hooks and have the characteristic hairwing which labels them as bucktails.

Many of these flies come from the United States, although a group of flies that I have had some success with are the Bucktail nymphs. I like to think of this group of flies as a 'Broad Spectrum' type of lure. By broad spectrum I mean that they are tied with no particular creature in mind, but are taken by the trout for whatever the trout wants them to be at that time. The black and white illustration shows the general shape of these flies and the dressings are just a guide, for one can appreciate that the combinations of colour are limitless. Other lures that use the tied-down hairwing are ones that are designed as 'shrimp' type imitations and differ from the bucktail nymphs in that they do not have the 'V' formation projecting out from the head. Many of the caddis fly imitations given in the chapter on dry fly lures can be fished wet as larva imitations.

The Bucktail Nymphs

Black

> BODY.   Black seal fur.
> RIB.   Oval silver tinsel.
> TAIL AND BACK.   Black bucktail or squirrel, the roots projecting over the head in a divided 'V'.

Fig. 33   Bucktail Nymph

Brown

> BODY.   Fiery brown seal fur.
> RIB.   Oval gold tinsel.
> TAIL AND BACK.   Natural brown bucktail.

White

> BODY.   White seal fur.
> RIB.   Oval silver tinsel.
> TAIL AND BACK.   White bucktail.

Grey Squirrel

> BODY.   Hare's ear.
> RIB.   Oval gold.
> TAIL AND BACK.   Grey squirrel.

Red Squirrel

> BODY.   Grey under fur.

RIB. Oval gold tinsel.

TAIL AND BACK. Natural red squirrel.

Caddis Larva

BODY. Brown floss silk tied around the bend of the hook.

WING AND HACKLE. A light spinning of deer hair tied sloping backward beyond the hook.

This last pattern can have a varied body colour, brown, green, yellow, through to red, and is a popular pattern for the swift flowing rivers of the American West.

The Picket Pin (as tied by the Orvis Co.)

TAIL. Light red game fibres pointing downward.

BODY. Bronze peacock herl.

HACKLE. Palmered red game.

WING. Grey squirrel.

HEAD. Bronze peacock herl.

The Picket Pin when fished slowly along the reservoir or river bottom makes a very good imitation of the larval stage of the larger aquatic beetles or even the predatory dragonfly nymph.

The following two patterns are tied to represent shrimps; the first is an American pattern, the other is a Black Shrimp tied by Dave Shewan of Aberdeen and is a successful pattern for salmon and seatrout.

Grey Shrimp

BODY. Grey fur.

RIB. Silver oval tinsel.

TAIL AND BACK. Grey squirrel tail (tied down at rear and head).

HEAD. Black (sometimes painted with an eye).

Black Shrimp (Shewan)

BODY. Black ostrich herl.

BELLY.   Flat strip of silver tinsel or lurex.
TAIL AND BACK.   Black hackle fibres or black squirrel (tied down).

Having sneaked a couple of shrimps into this chapter it would be unfair not to include the succulent crayfish.

Those of us lucky enough to fish waters with a high alkaline content may well come across this mini freshwater lobster. Eaten for its own sake by us humans, it provides a cordon bleu meal fit for kings and gourmets. It also provides such a meal for large trout and the wily chub, in fact both species of fish relish the crayfish as food. Where permissible it is a good idea to use the natural creature as live bait, but on 'fly only' waters a lure to imitate the creature must be resorted to.

The first bucktail lure comes from the United States and is an impression of an American Crayfish in mating finery.

Crayfish

BODY.   Silver.
WING.   Orange bucktail, green bucktail.
UNDER WING.   White bucktail.

Many times I have moved logs or large stones from the river to see these small olive green creatures scuttling backwards into dark corners, some were over four inches, others mere babies. It was one of these babies that I took home and kept alive in a gold-fish bowl in an endeavour to represent the same in fur or feather. The results of my labours were two lures, both of which subsequently caught both chub, albeit small ones, and reasonable sized trout.

The first fly is a straightforward bucktail fly resembling the crayfish in colour only. The second is a more direct copy of the natural creature.

Crayfish Bucktail

BODY.   Green seal fur.

RIB.   Gold oval tinsel.

WING.   Divided green bucktail (splay wing) extending well
beyond the end of the hook.

UNDER BODY.   Olive cock a little lighter than the wing,
though not important.

CHEEK.   Long jungle cock to the end of hook.

Crayfish

UNDER BODY.   Copper wire with floss silk over.

BODY.   Deer hair dyed or coloured green and then clipped
to shape. Dark green Raffene over the back.

RIB.   Fluorescent green silk over the back.

TAIL.   Olive cock fibres tied pointing down.

CLAWS.   Tied in at the head in a 'V' green bucktail.

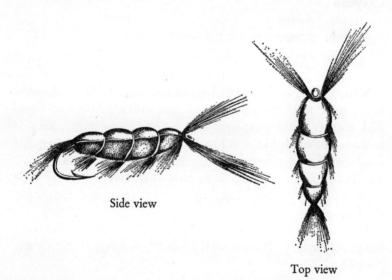

Side view

Top view

Fig. 34   Crayfish Lure

For the latter fly the step by step procedure for tying is as follows:

1. Wind silk from head to tail, then a spiral of copper wire, followed by floss silk.
2. Tie in tail.
3. Tie in ribbing silk at the tail end.
4. Tie in Raffene at the tail end.
5. Coat body with Venglaze polyurethane varnish.
6. Spin on deer hair to the head leaving room for bucktail claws.
7. Clip deer hair to shape over back and sides leaving the underneath unclipped, but thin out to resemble legs.
8. Damp the Raffene and stretch over the back, tie in at the head.
9. Wind the ribbing silk in widening segments, tie in at the head.
10. Tie in a bunch of bucktail forward over the head, the roots treated with Venglaze.
11. Divide the hair into a 'V' with a figure 8 whip.
12. Whip finish and apply varnish.

This fly, tied in a variety of colours from natural to orange, makes a reasonable representation of a prawn for both salmon and sea fishing.

Crayfish should be fished deep and retrieved very slowly with occasional spurts, for best effect.

[13]

Frogs and Tadpoles

Some eyebrows will be raised at the thought of tying flies to imitate the amphibians, although these creatures do have some prominence as food for more than one species of fish.

In the old days frogs were considered a good livebait for pike, though, for the life of me, how any one could stick a hook into these inoffensive creatures beats me. Frogs too are considered excellent fare for large and small mouth bass in the United States.

Land reclamation and urban development, not to mention the indiscriminate use of lethal insecticides, herbicides and other environmental suicides on our farm lands, has sadly depleted the frog population of this country. At least we are now aware of this and can only hope that we are not too late in saving the little green croakers from complete extinction.

While fishing a reservoir in southern England last season I noticed at my feet long gelatinous fronds of toad spawn. In my childhood every self-respecting boy who sought sticklebacks in jam jars also collected annually the tapioca spawn of frogs to watch the metamorphosis of spawn to tadpole to adult frog. Where frogs and toads still exist and are evident in the water it is a good idea to fish representations of both the tadpole and adult frog to lure both trout and savage pike.

Tadpole Streamer (Price)
> BODY. This also includes the head, either bulky Black Chenille or clipped deer hair coloured afterwards with a black felt-tipped pen.

HACKLE.   Tied behind the head and body . . . a sparse black
hen hackle.

WINGS.   These are in effect the tail of the tadpole, two black
hen hackles back to back extending well beyond the hook.

When using clipped deer hair it is advisable to weight the hook
by means of copper wire.

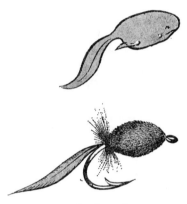

Fig. 35   Tadpole and Streamer

This fly should be fished in yard long pulls and by jerking the
rod to impart that enticing wriggle of the natural tadpole.

So remember; when tadpoles are about in your particular
water try the Tadpole Streamer, it may well make the difference
between a good and a mediocre catch.

The adult frog is a different matter. This is represented as a
surface lure. Many such lures are sold in America as 'Deer Hair'
bugs for bass fishing, but there is no earthly reason why the same
lure should not capture large trout and good-sized pike. Though
not strictly a lure of the streamer and bucktail family, or even a
fish-simulating lure like the polystickle, I felt it worth including
for its own sake, without having to include a further chapter on bass
bugs and popping lures which have not as yet caught on in this
country to any extent.

Surface Frog Lure

BODY.   Clipped deer hair coloured with waterproof felt-
tipped pens. Green on the top, yellow on the bottom.

LEGS.   Green bucktail for the front legs, yellow for the back,
or a mixture of both.

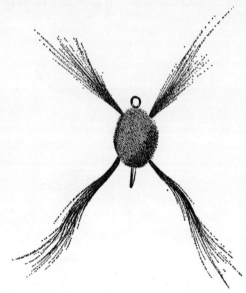

Fig. 36   Floating Frog Lure

The back legs are slightly longer than the forelegs.

Fished on the surface along the reed fringes, and giving the lure
plenty of rod action to move the legs, it should provide a killing
lure for both trout and pike at dusk, and also for those large chub
who are not averse to taking frogs when the opportunity occurs.

The cousin of the frog is the newt. This creature can easily be
represented by a Matuka style of fly and fished below the surface,
the peculiar winging of the Matuka dressing resembling the crested
back of the newt.

[14]

Salmon

Time and time again we read in the angling publications theories regarding the salmon's feeding or, more precisely, the non-feeding habits, in freshwater. 'The salmon never feeds in freshwater'. 'The salmon only feeds on minute freshwater creatures'. 'The salmon regurgitates its stomach contents when hooked'.

The truth of the matter is, fortunately for we anglers, that salmon can be taken on worms, sprats, plugs, spinners, wet flies, dry flies and even minute flies meant for trout.

Why does a salmon take a lure, fly etc. if it does not feed in freshwater? Can we assume that the salmon is under the misapprehension that it is still in the sea? It could account for the success of natural baits such as prawns, sprats etc.

Does the salmon take from anger or pique? Or is there in its tiny brain a vestige of memory left from its parr days, that recognises in, shall we say a Black Gnat, a tasty morsel? Who can tell. I have seen salmon ignore a range of flies, look with disdain on the most exciting of spinners, only to rise and engulf a cigarette packet. What a perverse creature it can be. There are times when the gaudiest of flies or brightest of spinners will attract the fish, and at others the minutest natural insect floating over its lie will send it into shudders of fright and into the darkness of the deep water.

The great American angler Lee Wulff in his book *The Atlantic Salmon*, states that the salmon is reluctant to take a streamer fly on most occasions. However he does admit that there are times when this type of fly will succeed when all others have failed. I am of the opinion that any fish that can be taken on a spinner will fall to the allure of a properly presented streamer fly. Reading through books and past editions of various angling publications, time and time again I have found accounts of good fish caught, and exciting days spent using streamer flies, too numerous to be the occasional fluke.

Tandem lures have at times accounted for good fish. Lures such as the Red Terror, Norsk Lure and even the ubiquitous Black Lure all have been and still can be effective. Mention has already been made of the sixteen salmon caught in Ireland on a Grafham Grey Lure.

Bucktail or Hairwing? A bucktail is a hairwing and vice versa. In the U.S.A. they are inevitably referred to as Bucktail Salmon

Fig. 37 'Rat' Bucktail

Flies. If a difference must be made then one could make it in the type of hook used, i.e. a hairwing would be tied on a conventional salmon hook and a bucktail tied on a strong heavy wire long shank hook. Also the bucktail perhaps has a longer wing extending beyond the bend of the hook and the hairwing's wing to the bend, but the difference is so small that for the purpose of this book of dressings I make no differentiation.

The following list of dressings are but a few of the current flies in use on both sides of the Atlantic for the lordly salmon. Many of the American patterns were kindly sent to me by The Orvis Company of Vermont. I was always under the misapprehension that commercial flies in the United States were not up to much. The sample flies sent by Orvis proved how wrong I could be.

The 'Rat' series of Bucktails, as tied by Orvis Company Ltd:

The Rusty Rat

TAG. Fine gold wire.

TAIL. Green peacock sword herl.

BODY. Two-thirds yellow floss silk, one-third peacock herl beneath the wing.

WING. A strip of yellow body floss extending to end of tail. Mixed brown and white hair over (mixed red and grey squirrel).

HACKLE. Collar style, soft long fibred grizzle.

Silver Rat

TAG. None.

TAIL. None.

BODY. Embossed silver tinsel.

WING. Grey hair (grey squirrel).

HACKLE. Collar style, soft long fibred grizzle.

Grey Rat

TAG. Silver wire.

TAIL. None.

BODY. Grey wool or fur.

RIB. Silver oval.

WING. Grey hair (grey squirrel).

HACKLE. Collar style, soft long fibred grizzle.

Black Rat

TAG. Gold oval tinsel.

TAIL. None.

BODY. Bronze peacock herl.

WING. Black hair (black squirrel).

HACKLE. Collar style, soft long fibred grizzle.

Brown Rat

TAG. Two turns flat gold tinsel followed by golden yellow floss butt.

TAIL. Green peacock sword herl.

BODY. Brown floss silk.

RIB.   Fine gold oval.

WING.   Mixed brown and white hair (red and grey squirrel mixed).

HACKLE.   Collar style, long fibred grizzle,

Some of the original 'Rat' dressings called for a wing of grey fox pelt. However the grey fox fur is a little difficult to come by in this country so the various winging mediums given should suffice. I would indeed be surprised if a salmon turned down the fly because the wing was of squirrel rather than fox.

The Rusty and Silver Rat were mentioned by Charles Ritz in his book *A Fly Fisher's Life*, as flies that he now includes in his fly box. They were brought to his attention whilst fishing in Scandinavia.

The following American pattern is a successful lure for most species of game fish.

Cosseboom

TAG.   Flat silver tinsel.

TAIL.   Green floss silk (light colour).

BODY.   Green floss as for tail.

RIB.   Oval or flat tinsel.

WING.   Grey squirrel.

HACKLE.   Collar style, yellow.

This last pattern also occurs in Donald Dubois' book *The Fisherman's Handbook of Trout Flies* where three versions are given. Some books give the pattern as having a red head, others black.

The next fly is another trout pattern that has made the successful transition to salmon fishing.

McGregor Bucktail

TAG.   (Optional). Flat silver tinsel.

TAIL.   Golden pheasant crest.

BODY.   Orange chenille.

RIB.   Silver tinsel.

WING.   Grey squirrel.

CHEEK.   Jungle cock.

HACKLE.   Under hackle grizzle.

Salmon Muddler

This is the famous Muddler Minnow in exactly the same dressing as given in the Muddler chapter. However for the salmon pattern a double hook is usually used.

The following fly is probably the best known British streamer pattern for salmon, just as many trout patterns are used for big brother salmon. I have seen this fly used with great success on reservoirs for rainbow trout.

Fig. 38   Elver Lure

The Elver Fly

BODY.   Black floss.

RIB.   Silver flat tinsel.

WING.   Blue Vulturine guinea fowl feathers (with white centre stripe).

HACKLE.   Blue guinea fowl feather (not striped).

Another British salmon fly pattern which to my mind falls into the streamer style like the Elver fly, is the Welsh version of the Shrimp Fly.

The Welsh Shrimp Fly

TAG.   Yellow floss silk.

TAIL.   Golden pheasant crest feather.

BUTT.   Black ostrich herl.

BODY.   Yellow floss silk.

RIB.   Oval silver tinsel.

WING. Golden pheasant body feathers (red), back to back over the body.
CHEEK. Jungle cock.
HACKLE. (Collar style) white cock.

The 'Hairwing/Bucktail' salmon flies are making ever-increasing inroads into the realm of the older more traditional salmon flies. These simple lures appear to be accounting for many fish and a greater number of anglers are turning over to these easier to construct lures. The following list of dressings are but a few in use on our rivers today. Many of the traditional built wing salmon flies are now being dressed using hair as the integral part of the wing. These are not included in this book.

Hairy Mary

TAIL. Golden pheasant crest.
BODY. Black floss silk.
RIB. Oval silver tinsel.
WING. Dark brown bucktail.
HACKLE. Dark blue.

A further version of the above which has proved quite successful on occasions is the Blue Mary, due to the soft nature of the lurex it is advisable to coat with several layers of clear varnish.

Blue Mary

TAIL. Golden pheasant crest.
BODY. Blue lurex heavily varnished.
RIB. Silver oval.
WING. Intermixed black and blue bucktail.
HACKLE. Dark blue.

Garry

TAG. Silver tinsel and yellow floss.
TAIL. Red ibis and golden pheasant crest.
BODY. Black floss.
RIB. Oval silver rib.

WING. Yellow bucktail, few strands red bucktail beneath.
HACKLE. Blue Galena (Guinea fowl).

W. J. Davidson of Davidson Flies, Fraserburgh, Aberdeenshire, sent me the following hairwing salmon flies which have proven very successful for the last few years. They are patterns exclusive to the above company, and the samples sent to me are a fine example of the fly dresser's art.

Black Orbe

TAIL. Golden pheasant crest.
TAG. Oval silver wire.
BODY. Black floss silk.
RIB. Oval silver wire.
HACKLE. False hackle of black hen or cock.
WING. Black squirrel, golden pheasant topping over.
SIDES. Two strands of peacock herl extending just beyond the hook.

Perfecta

TAIL. Golden pheasant crest.
BODY. Gold and silver tinsel.
HACKLE. False hackle of light blue cock or hen.
WING. Red squirrel, golden pheasant topping over.

Golden Buck

TAIL. Golden pheasant tippets.
TAG. Gold oval.
BODY. Flat gold tinsel, oval gold rib.
HACKLE. False hackle of ginger or natural light red cock.
WING. Red squirrel.

Cavalier

TAIL. Short tuft of red wool.
TAG. Two turns of oval silver tinsel.
BODY. Flat silver tinsel, oval silver tib.
HACKLE. False hackle of light blue cock.
WING. Black squirrel, topping over.

Father Time
TAIL.   Golden pheasant crest.
TAG.   Three turns of oval gold tinsel.
BODY.   Flat gold tinsel oval silver rib.
HACKLE.   False hackle of yellow cock.
WING.   Black squirrel.
CHEEK.   Two whole golden pheasant tippet feathers either side.

Mimosa
TAIL.   Golden pheasant crest.
TAG.   Three turns oval silver tinsel.
BODY.   In two halves, the rear half flat silver tinsel, oval silver rib. Second half . . . black floss silk oval gold rib.
HACKLE.   False hackle bright yellow cock.
WING.   Black squirrel.

The following fly needs no introduction in the form below, and as a tube fly it has accounted for many salmon.

Stoats Tail
TAIL.   None.
BODY.   Black floss.
RIB.   Silver tinsel.
WING.   Stoat's tail in smaller versions, black squirrel in larger flies.
HACKLE.   Sparse under hackle of black cock.

Bourach
TAIL.   None.
BODY.   Embossed silver tinsel.
WING.   Light blue bucktail.
UNDER WING.   Yellow bucktail.

David Shewan, professional fly dresser of Aberdeen, sent me the following excellent fish catching patterns for the Nith.

Copper Stoat (Low water fly)
    TAG.   Copper tinsel.
    TAIL.   Golden pheasant crest.
    BODY.   Embossed copper tinsel.
    WING.   Stoat tail.
    HACKLE.   Very dark blue (sparse).
    HEAD.   Black.

Brownie
    TAG.   Gold tinsel flat.
    TAIL.   Golden pheasant crest and blue galena fibres.
    BODY.   Neutral grey floss.
    RIB.   Fine embossed copper tinsel.
    WING.   Brown bucktail.
    HACKLE.   Soft grizzle (sparse).
    HEAD.   Black.

The following pattern is derived from a trout fly of the same name and is used a great deal on Canadian waters.

Grizzly King
    TAG.   Round silver tinsel.
    TAIL.   Dyed red swan.
    BODY.   Green floss silk.
    RIB.   Oval silver tinsel.
    WING.   Mixed brown and white bucktail.
    HACKLE.   Collar style grizzle.

Martinez & Bird Ltd. of Redditch, Worcestershire kindly gave me permission to use the following dressing of a fly sent to them by Leslie Paterson (Alexandria) of Bearsden, Dumbartonshire. They call this fly Evening Glow because it includes in its make up a fluorescent tag.

Evening Glow
    TAG.   Green fluorescent wool.
    BODY.   Embossed silver tinsel.

WING. Dyed yellow squirrel tail.
CHEEK. Jungle cock.
HACKLE. White cock.

A variation of the Stoat Tail is the Orange Thunder Stoat. Mention of this was made by Tom Stewart in his column 'Popular Flies' in *Trout and Salmon*.

Orange Thunder Stoat
TAG. Oval silver tinsel.
TAIL. Golden pheasant crest.
BODY. Black floss silk.
RIB. Fine oval gold tinsel.
WING. Black squirrel.
CHEEK. Jungle cock.
HACKLE. Orange cock hackle fibres, beard fashion.

The following fly, like the Grizzly King is another popular Canadian pattern for the Atlantic salmon.

Red Abbey
TAG. Round silver tinsel.
TAIL. Dyed red swan or goose.
BODY. Red floss silk.
RIB. Flat silver tinsel.
WING. Brown squirrel or bucktail.
HACKLE. Light brown collar style.

Brown Bomber (Canadian)
TAG. Flat silver tinsel, followed by yellow floss.
TAIL. Golden pheasant crest.
BODY. Brown seal fur or wool.
RIB. Oval silver tinsel.
WING. Red squirrel.
CHEEK. Jungle cock.
HACKLE. False hackle very sparse, brown.

Black Bomber (Canadian)

TAG.   Silver tinsel and yellow floss.
TAIL.   Golden pheasant crest.
BODY.   Black seals fur or wool.
RIB.   Oval silver tinsel.
WING.   Black squirrel.
CHEEK.   Jungle cock.
HACKLE.   Sparse black.

Grey Bomber (Canadian)

TAG.   Silver tinsel and yellow floss.
TAIL.   Golden pheasant crest.
BODY.   Flat silver tinsel.
RIB.   Oval silver tinsel.
WING.   Brown and white bucktail.
CHEEK.   Jungle cock.
HACKLE.   Guinea fowl sparse.

The Bomber series of flies are often dressed with a butt of black chenille and sometimes with an over topping of golden pheasant crest.

Yellow Goshawk (British)

TAG.   Oval gold tinsel.
TAIL.   Mixed golden pheasant crest, red ibis and barred teal.
BODY.   Black seal fur or, picked out black wool.
RIB.   Oval gold tinsel.
WING.   Yellow bucktail.
HACKLE.   False claret cock.

Black Bear (U.S.A.)

TAG.   Oval gold tinsel.
TAIL.   Golden pheasant crest or black hackle fibres.
BODY.   Black seal fur or wool.
RIB.   Oval gold tinsel.
WING.   Black bear or squirrel.
HACKLE.   False hackle black cock or hair as wing.

Black Bear Orange Butt

TAG.   Oval gold tinsel.
TAIL.   Black hackle fibres.
BUTT.   Fluorescent orange tag.
BODY.   Black seal fur or wool.
RIB.   Oval gold tinsel.
WING.   Black bear or squirrel.
HACKLE.   Sparse black cock or black hair as wing.

Black Bear Green Butt

As above with fluorescent green butt.

Black Dragon (British)

TAIL.   Black squirrel tail.
BODY.   Black wool or chenille.
RIB.   Embossed silver tinsel.
WING.   Black squirrel.
HACKLE.   Black cock collar.

Hot Orange (U.S.A.)

TAG.   Flat gold tinsel.
TAIL.   Golden pheasant crest.
BUTT.   Yellow floss.
BODY.   Black floss.
RIB.   Gold oval tinsel.
WING.   Black squirrel or bucktail.
HACKLE.   Hot orange cock.

Bill's Badger (British)

BODY.   Black floss (thin).
RIB.   Flat silver tinsel.
WING.   Badger hair.
HACKLE.   Dark blue cock.

Yellow Bucktail (U.S.A.)

TAIL.   Golden pheasant crest.
BODY.   Flat silver tinsel.

American Lures

FIRST AND SECOND ROWS
TIED BY THE KEEL FLY COMPANY OF TRAVERESE CITY MICHIGAN
Mickey Fin   Muddler Minnow   Royal Coachman
Bonesnook Special   Blacknosed Dace

THIRD ROW
Skykomish Sunrise Streamer (*Gapen Fly Company*)   Thief (*Gapen Fly Co.*) Trude

FOURTH AND FIFTH ROWS
WELL KNOWN AMERICAN PATTERNS TIED BY THE AUTHOR
Alaska Mary   Blue Damsel   Spruce
Sandborn Streamer   Cut Lips   Black Ghost

SIXTH ROW
BUCKTAIL SALMON FLIES TIED BY THE ORVIS COMPANY OF VERMONT
Brown Rat   Rusty Rat   Silver Rat   Black Rat

SEVENTH ROW
TERRESTRIAL FLIES TIED BY THE ORVIS COMPANY OF VERMONT
Letort Hopper   Bird's Stonefly   Letort cricket   Deerhopper

RIB. Oval silver tinsel.
WING. Yellow bucktail.
HACKLE. Yellow cock.

Lady Gwen (British)
TAG. Round silver tinsel.
TAIL. Golden pheasant crest.
BODY. Black floss silk.
RIB. Flat silver tinsel.
WING. Yellow dyed grey squirrel.
HACKLE. Black or dark blue.

Skunk Tail
TAG. Magenta fluorescent floss.
TAIL. Golden pheasant crest.
BODY. Black floss silk.
RIB. Oval silver tinsel.
WING. Dark skunk tail hair or black squirrel.
CHEEK. Jungle cock.
HACKLE. False black hackle sparse.

Dragon Lady (British)
TAIL. Golden pheasant crest.
BODY. Black chenille or wool.
RIB. Embossed silver tinsel.
WING. Grey squirrel.
CHEEK. Jungle cock.
HACKLE. Ginger cock collar style.

The Mickey Finn, the dressing for which was given in the chapter on 'Mylar' is also at times an effective pattern for salmon.

Mickey Finn
TAIL. None (though a yellow and red bucktail can be added).
BODY. Embossed silver tinsel or flat tinsel oval rib.
WING. Yellow, red and yellow bucktail.
CHEEK. Jungle cock.
HACKLE. None.

I

There is a well known dry fly pattern for salmon called The Pink Lady, however there is also a bucktail fly of the same name.

Pink Lady (U.S.A.)
TAG.   Fine oval tinsel.
TAIL.   Golden pheasant crest.
BODY.   In two halves, green tinsel and silver tinsel.
RIB.   Round silver tinsel.
WING.   Badger hair, pink hair over.
HACKLE.   Blue jay false hackle or dyed guinea fowl.

Like the well known Stoat Tail and Hairy Mary flies the following fly has many variations. John Veniard give five such variations in *A Further Guide to Fly Dressing*.

Stewart's Killer
TAIL.   Long red hackle fibres.
BODY.   Flat silver tinsel.
RIB.   Gold wire.
WING.   Stoat tail or black squirrel.
CHEEK.   Jungle cock.
HACKLE.   Natural red false hackle tied sparse.

Stewart's Orange Killer
As above but with an orange hackle.

Stewart's Blue Killer
As above but with a blue hackle.

Another American streamer that has proved successful over here for salmon is the Red Badger, this can be tied with or without jungle cock cheeks.

Red Badger
TAIL.   Dyed red swan or goose.
BODY.   Red wool.
RIB.   Flat gold tinsel.
WING.   Two badger hackles back to back.
CHEEK.   Jungle cock (optional).
HACKLE.   Collar style badger cock.

[15]

Seatrout

The streamer fly is used a great deal in the Western States of America for the Steelhead trout, the migratory cousin of the elegant Rainbow. The same can be true in this country, large streamers and bucktails can prove equally as attractive for our migratory trout, the Seatrout, Peal, Sewin, Finnock Salmon Trout, Whitling, White trout etc., etc. Such a lot of names for the sporting prince of game fish.

We in this country have used the long multi-hook lure for this game fish for many years, so it can be fair to say that the use of streamer type lures is not new to the British angler.

The seatrout is somewhat more predictable than the lordly disdainful salmon, and can be fished for in a greater number of places. The seatrout unlike the salmon can in fact be fly fished successfully in salt water and in the brackish water of our estuaries. However the further up the river the prodigal trout goes, and the longer it remains in the same, the more difficult it becomes to take it during the hours of daylight. Then the exciting sport of night fishing for seatrout comes into its own. Aficionados of seatrout fishing will tell you the only form of fishing for these fish is to seek them in the hours of darkness, ears cocked for the sound of the splash of a heavy fish that has shyly laid low all day, rising only at night to feed undisturbed.

Streamers, bucktails, tandem lures can be used to take the seatrout in all stages of its journey from the sea to the final spawning area.

Most patterns given in this book can at times be suitable for fishing for this fish, and it is not unknown for them to be taken on simple mackerel feathers in the estuaries of our rivers.

The following list of dressings are of flies that have proved successful for the capture of seatrout in many waters.

Spencer Bay Special
This blue-coloured American streamer has proved very effective for seatrout as well as for lake rainbows.

TAIL.   Golden pheasant tippets.
BODY.   Flat silver tinsel.
WINGS.   Two blue hackles back to back, two furnace hackles outside.
CHEEK.   Jungle cock.
HACKLE.   Mixed collar of blue and yellow cock.

Blue Flash
This streamer I devised for dusk and night fishing and is of a similar coloration to the above, with the exception of the red in the tail and hackle. Blue appears in many areas to be an attractive colour for seatrout.

TAIL.   Red hackle fibres (scarlet).
BODY.   White floss ribbed with pale fluorescent chenille.
WING.   Four blue hackles back to back.
CHEEK.   Jungle cock.
HACKLE.   Beard hackle of scarlet cock fibres.

Examples of the type of fly tied by Davidson flies of Fraserburgh were given in the last chapter on the Salmon, however they do not confine themselves just to the tying of salmon flies. Amongst the dressings and examples of their work sent to me were two very interesting and unusual seatrout lures, utilising a silver and gold tinsel for the wing. Mr. Davidson informs me that the flies are particularly effective for night fishing.

Davidson Star Fly Blue
TAIL.   None.
BODY.   Flat silver tinsel.
HACKLE.   Collar hackle of medium blue.

WING. Above and below hook and streaming beyond the bend of the hook gold and silver tinsel (one of the plastic tinsels).

Davidson Star Fly Green

TAIL. None.
BODY. Mixed gold and silver tinsel.
HACKLE. Collar hackle of green (green highlander shade).
WING. As above pattern.

A fly sent to me by Mr. I. G. Williams of Llanelli, Carmarthenshire is a bucktail pattern designed to take the famed Sewin of the principality. Mr. Williams has based his fly on the Jersey Herd, and a fly mentioned by Hugh Falkus called the 'Medicine Fly'. Because of its potential as a reservoir trout fly and its possibility as a salmon lure, Mr. Williams christened it the Allrounder.

The Allrounder (Williams)

TAIL. None.
BODY. Built up to a cigar shape with floss silk then covered with copper Lurex.
RIB. Oval gold tinsel.
HACKLE. False hackle of light blue cock, beneath the hackle a butt of mixed red and DFM magenta wool.
WING. Red squirrel.
HEAD. Black.

William M. Iveson, professional fly dresser from Brampton, Huntingdon, originally hailed from the Yorkshire/Westmoreland border country. Two flies that are popular in that district are the Veevers Fancy and a variant. Mr. Iveson gives the dressings for them as follows:

Veevers Fancy

HOOK. Normal shank.
TAIL. Golden pheasant crest.
TAG. Silver oval.

BODY. Flat silver tinsel.
RIB. Silver oval.
HACKLE. Yellow cock.
WING. Grey squirrel.
CHEEK. Jungle cock.
HEAD Black.

Veevers Fancy Variant

TAIL. Golden pheasant crest.
BODY. Yellow floss.
RIB. Oval gold tinsel.
HACKLE. Yellow cock.
WING. Grey squirrel.
CHEEK. Jungle cock.
HEAD. Black.

Another fly sent to me by Mr. Iveson is a low water seatrout fly which is reputed to be killing for the Sewin of Wales.

The Red Rib

HOOK. Tied on size 8 low water salmon hooks.
TAIL. Golden pheasant crest.
TAG. Copper wire.
BODY. Black wool.
RIB. Red lurex.
WING. Badger.
HACKLE. Yellow cock false hackle.

Badger and Silver

This fly is a popular fly for the Sewin of North Wales.

TAIL. None.
BODY. Flat silver tinsel.
WING AND HACKLE. Tied in brushwire, silver badger hair.

Skunk tail can be used as a substitute for the above fly and for the following variants.

Blue Badger
As Badger and Silver with additional blue collar hackle.

Red Badger
As above with red collar hackle.

Yellow Badger
As above with yellow hackle.

Orange Badger
As above with orange hackle.
   I have taken good rainbow and brown trout with the yellow and the orange patterns.

David Shewan's Estuary Streamers

White Silver Cheek
   TAIL.   Dyed red hackle fibres.
   BODY.   Blue flat tinsel.
   WING.   Two white cock hackles flanking the hook shank and four or five strands of silver Luron approx $\frac{1}{16}$ in wide.

Black Silver Cheek
   TAIL.   Dyed red hackle fibres.
   BODY.   Flat blue tinsel.
   WING.   Two black cock hackles flanking body.
   CHEEK.   Two strips of Luron the length of the wing $\frac{3}{8}$ in wide.

Grey Silver Cheek
   TAIL.   Red hackle fibres.
   BODY.   Flat silver tinsel fine silver rib.
   WING.   Two badger hackles flanking the body.
   CHEEK.   Two strips of Luron the length of the wing $\frac{3}{8}$ in wide.

Silver Nylon Silver Cheek
   TAIL.   Dyed red hackle fibres.
   BODY.   Flat gold or silver tinsel.

WING AND UNDERBODY. Mixed strands of white nylon filaments and strips of fine Luron $\frac{1}{16}$ wide.

John Veniard gives the following dressing in his book *A Further Guide to Fly Dressing* for a Danish Streamer for Seatrout.

Silver Badger Streamer
TAIL.   None.
BODY.   Flat silver tinsel.
WING.   Badger hackles back to back.
HACKLE.   Collar style badger hackle.

The following fly was devised in the Western States of America for Steelhead fishing. In this country it has proved its worth for seatrout and also for grilse.

Golden Demon
TAIL.   Golden pheasant crest.
BODY.   Flat gold tinsel.
RIB.   Oval gold tinsel.
WING.   Brown bucktail.
CHEEK.   Jungle cock.
HACKLE.   Orange.

As in the last chapter on salmon patterns, mention was made of the Muddler Minnow. Needless to say it has proved a very effective way of taking seatrout especially during the daylight hours, dressed fairly lightly and fished as both a surface and sub-surface lure.

Many of the patterns given in the chapter on Sea Flies can be used successfully for the seatrout in esturine waters, after all the small fish that these flies represent have been the food for the sea-trout during its sojourn in the salt sea.

[16]

Lure Fishing Methods

There is no great deal of difference between fishing lures or conventional flies, the biggest secret is to remember that the feathers and fur at the end of your leader is a small fish, a bizarre strange coloured fish perhaps, but a fish nevertheless. Always give movement to the lure by moving the rod, varying the speed of retrieve and by changing the direction of the lure from time to time.

STILLWATER

The term stillwater embraces the modern man made reservoirs, the beautiful lochs and loughs of Scotland and Ireland, and even the small tarns and ponds scattered the length and breadth of the country.

Methods evolved for fishing one type of water can be utilised for any other as situations dictate, even though most waters have an individual character. One of the biggest problems facing a tyro when he first takes up stillwater fly fishing is the expanse of water. Where to fish? It is a matter of fact that a casual day ticket holder will never be as successful as a local, who by trial and error, observation and knowledge of the lake or reservoir, has noted the best fish holding spots. He may well also know where the last restocking took place, which can be useful, if not a little unfair.

Always ask the resident bailiff when in doubt, advice is always freely given for it is in his interest that you catch fish. That is what he is there for.

An angler too can help himself by observation of the natural topography. In the formation of reservoirs, land is submerged, under water with this land are hedgerows, roads, even houses, walls and dykes. All of these become good fish holding areas. Around the perimeter of such waters, vestiges of the roads, tracks and hedges remain and the angler can follow them into the reservoir itself. Such places afford a productive larder for the trout, the remains of hedges swarm with shrimp, nymph and small fry.

The dam wall also can provide a good fishing area, large trout cruise up and down feeding, and where it is allowed the apron of the dam is a good place to fish. Any inflow of water is yet again a good fishing area, even the slightest trickle of water entering the lake can provide the trout with a flow of food or perhaps a better temperature level than the rest of the lake or reservoir especially in warm weather.

As the season progresses (during the hours of daylight) the fish are driven further from the bank due to the noise and splashing and general mêlée of bank activity. It is then that the exponent of the shooting head comes into its own. There are many books that explain the techniques of casting quite fully.

STILLWATER METHODS

Chasing Minnow
This method relies on the theory that the trout are induced to take either the minnow representation or the smaller nymph type flies, that it appears to be chasing. I like to think this is so. However Al McClane, the fishing editor of *Field and Stream* in his book *Practical Fly Fishing*, mentions this technique but doubts whether the trout do in fact think that the streamer is a small fish chasing its dinner. Dave Colyer wrote on the same theme a few years back, on how he was shown this method at Weirwood, and it successfully caught fish when all other methods failed. Soon after reading this article I tried it for myself and took three rainbows in quick succession from a spot that an angler had vacated, not having had a touch for over an hour. On that occasion I used a Black and Orange Marabou on the point chasing two corixa flies on the droppers. This team I fished fairly quickly with short pauses before recovering more line. Two trout took the larger Marabou Streamer and one fell to the corixa.

Nymphing Trout

There are occasions when the trout during the evening rise slash
and attack nymphs emerging from the shucks, quite often the
angler can match the hatch as it were and collect one or two trout
during the frenzied evening rise. There are times however when
no matter what we try, all artificial nymphs and dry flies are
treated with utter disdain. 'I'm trying a size twenty' you hear
someone cry. 'The trout just come and have a look at it, and turn
away.' A garish streamer cast clumsily into the activity quite
often will take a fish. It may be due to the fact that the trout in their
eagerness to seize the juicy nymphs treat the streamer or bucktail
as an interloper and slash at it in anger.

When even this rather doubtful method fails I usually resort to
a pipe of tobacco and watch the rise until it wanes. Then I resort
to a streamer fly or lure, as it is approaching darkness the pattern
is of little consequence so a Black Lure is as good as any at such a
time. Fished fairly quickly the lure will often take one or two
trout in quick succession. This has worked for me time and time
again, and resultant autopsies on the trout reveal a surfeit of
nymph. It is as though the trout hang around awhile mopping up
the odd stray nymph and are tempted to take something different
that swims into their path. I find that the lure fished in yard long
pulls with occasional spurts, and the cast fished right into the bank,
achieves the best results.

Sticklebacking Trout

All of us have witnessed the furious attack of large trout on the
shoals of small fish that swim around the margins of the lake or
reservoirs. Not all of us however have witnessed the volcanic
eruption of small minnows from the surface of the water that is
often depicted in angling books. The trout seem to throw all
caution to the wind and come close into shore regardless of anglers.
With such lack of caution it should be easy to take trout after
trout but somehow this does not occur. I think the reason for this
is that most of us in our eagerness to get to grips with the trout,
fish our lures at too great a speed. When the trout slash and attack

the shoal or fry etc. they do not charge in, mouth wide open, engulfing small fish after small fish in much the same way as a whale, though I have seen this illustrated in one book. On the contrary the trout stun the fish in the fury of the attack, then they leisurely mop up the stunned and wounded trout in their own good time. Therefore a streamer cast out during a sticklebacking attack, then allowed to sink slowly to the bottom, then recovered in short one foot pulls will yield the angler a fair share of the predatory trout. The take can come when the fly is slowly sinking, static on the bottom or during the recovery.

Another method which can be utilised at such a time is the floating minnow. This can be an effective method especially in the shallows where much of the sticklebacking slaughter takes place. The streamer is constructed in such a way as to make it float, i.e. clipped deer hair body, or bodies constructed with an underbody of polyurethane foam. The fly is cast to the activity and allowed to float on the surface and twitched into life by uplifting the rod. This can be an exciting method of taking trout.

Buoyant Lure

Early in the season the trout lie deep near the bottom, a good method to tempt them is to use the buoyant lure on a sinking line for deep water. The theory being that the sinking line takes the fly down, but due to its natural buoyancy the fly is suspended in the water. On recovery, this should be in long steady pulls with pauses in between, the fly moves in a downward direction, during the pauses the fly flutters back up to its original position. On a floating line the introduction of a small lead shot on the cast achieves the same effect, and by varying where the shot is placed one can alter the position of the fly in relation to the bottom of the lake or reservoir.

Boat Techniques

Conventional methods of fly fishing from a boat also apply to streamer and bucktail flies, the only difference being the fly is larger.

Moving Boat

In an oar-propelled boat, providing someone else is doing the rowing, it is possible to take good fish by casting toward the shore and toward good fish holding areas, such as water inlets, weed patches etc. By casting your lure, at right angles to the boat, to such places you will find that on retrieve the lure is fished in a wide arc towards the rear of the boat. By continually fishing and retrieving and with the natural direction of the boat, a great deal of water can be covered.

Semi Dapping

This technique requires the angler to fish with the drift of the boat, and using a very long leader of about 15–20 feet. To cope with this long leader a long rod is a must. This method combines a dapping technique with the chasing minnow mentioned earlier. This works equally well with conventional flies as with streamers, but I prefer to fish a streamer at the point, followed by a nymph pattern on the lower dropper and a buzzy dry fly, or even a small muddler on the top dropper. The flies are cast ahead of the boat into the drift, with a minimum or no fly line in the water. By raising the rod from the horizontal to almost vertical causes the top fly to skitter back through the wavelets, the nymph to be fished just below the surface, and the streamer pattern to be below this. The larger streamer pattern is useful in allowing the two above flies to behave as stated above, smaller conventional flies have a tendency to rise to the surface and all three flies are virtually on the surface. This need not be a bad thing on occasions, but I believe that the natural progression of sub-surface, in the surface, and on the surface far more killing.

Vicinity of the Dam

When the wind is blowing toward the dam, causing the water to lap in waves on to the apron, it is a good idea to anchor the boat within casting distance of the apron, or if you are fortunate to have a rower, cast your streamer lure right up to the apron. A keel-type hook and a heavily dressed deer hair type fly is ideal for this situation as hook points can be broken. Always check the point of the hook. Retrieve your lure through the broken water into the quieter area in a fairly fast recovery. This method is also successful when waves have lapped at the edges of the bank causing a muddy area. Cast into this coloured area and retrieve the lure in steady yard pulls.

Trolling

On most British reservoirs trolling is not allowed, it is considered too killing a method of taking newly introduced stock trout, and due to the fact that there are never enough boats to go around, any bank anglers who may well remain fishless after a hard days fishing would justifiably be annoyed to see boat anglers take limit bags by trolling up and down water just out of their reach.

However on many of the Scottish and Irish natural lakes trolling is considered a normal method of taking large trout.

Trolling is the trailing behind a rowed or powered boat of a lure or fly. Fish can be taken by trolling methods at all depths, close to the surface or down near the bottom. Your conventional fly tackle can be used, or spinning tackle with monofilament or metal line. The latter when the trout are known to be at a very great depth. Both trout and salmon are sought by trolling methods and on some lakes with access to the sea large seatrout are often taken. In the past it was more usual to use spinners and plug type lures rather than streamer and bucktail flies, but such flies can be equally as killing. Multi hook tandem lures are particularly good for this style of fishing, over weedy areas keel type hooks are useful, marabou lures or any streamer with plenty of wing action are very attractive to the large trout. Many of the older books on fishing advise the use of a flat stone to hold down the line from the reel and to slow down the strike of the fish. If you are trolling on your own another method of doing this without a stone is to loop some line from the reel around your knee, it gives you that little extra time to drop the oars and grab the rod and strike home the hook.

As stated, flies can be fished at all depths, weighted flies, or extra weight on the line for deep trolling, no weight for just under the surface. The speed of trolling can be varied as can the distance of the fly from the boat, anything from 10–80 feet from the rod top.

A spinner/streamer combination can also be used for trolling.

Streamer and Bucktails in Fast Water

It is fairly true to say that streamers etc. are fished in this country mostly on modern reservoirs. However in the United States the highest proportion of streamer flies were designed to be fished in the fast river water, the greater proportion for the fast flowing wild rivers of the Western States.

Like normal flies, our lures can be fished upstream, downstream, and across the rivers as conditions dictate.

Again the important thing to remember is that in the main the lure we are using is an imitation of a small fish and must be fished as such.

Unlike stillwater fishing, movement is given to the fly by the natural current of the river, not by the angler. In lakes, to achieve lifelike action the angler resorts to moving his rod, and by varying the rate of line recovery. The river itself gives much of this movement to the fly.

Size and colour of the fly has already been discussed in earlier chapters, all that has been said should aid the angler in choosing the right fly for the water in the conditions that prevail.

Trout, salmon, seatrout and pike can be taken in rivers, some of the methods mentioned in the stillwater section can also apply to the river. Early in the season when the water is high, the buoyant fly technique can be used, as can the casting of the lure into the fish holding places where a tiny stream enters a main river. Sometimes when the river is in flood and highly coloured there are occasions when a feeder stream may well rise at a place unaffected by the rainfall that caused the main river to rise in muddy flood. The water of the feeder stream may well be clear, at such an ingress into the main river our quarry can be sought.

Upstream Streamer

Trout take up station in a river, where it can expend the minimum of energy and where a steady stream of food is brought down to it.

Such places would be large stones, a bend in the river, a semi-submerged log or perhaps a bank-fall promontory sticking out into the main stream. By careful wading and casting the lure just above such a boulder and to one side, recovering line quickly to keep the lure looking as natural as possible, good trout can be taken. Search the eddies either side of the boulder before moving on to the next possible trout station. What is needed in upstream streamer fishing is stealth, a short line, and quick line recovery.

Down Stream

In down stream fishing the streamer or bucktail lure must simulate a small fish struggling against the current. In the long riffles fish the fly accordingly with short jerky pulls and pauses in between.

Downstream and Static

To a dry fly purist or the addict of the upstream nymph the following method of taking fish will appear as only a little better than poaching or fishing with a worm. Nevertheless it catches fish. This method again relies on the fact that our streamer is a small fish making its way upstream against the current. Admittedly the amount of skill required in manipulating this method is such that a chimpanzee with very little training could accomplish the desired result in a very short time.

First cast the streamer down into a holding pool of quieter water and allow the fly to sink slowly by keeping the rod in the horizontal position. Step two is to slowly raise the rod, this has a tendency to make the streamer advance forward and rise a little higher in the water. Step three is once more to lower the rod to the almost horizontal, causing the streamer to fall back and deeper in the water. Step four is to recover about two foot of line then steps two, three and four continued until the fly has left the pool and has entered the faster water.

Fixed Line and Across

This again is another simple method of fishing the streamer fly. The fly is cast up and across to the fish holding area, if the angler is right handed. His left hand for once in his life can remain idle, for enough line is stripped off initially to reach the lie and no more is required. The line is cast as stated to the lie, but only allowed to remain in the water until the drag of the river takes effect. The line is then lifted off the water and recast to the same area. There are times when this method will put down every fish in the river, but there are occasions when the fish can be so angered at seeing the fly then having it snatched from him that it begins to wait for the next appearance of the strange vanishing fish, that it is oft times prompted to take from sheer frustration and anger.

Floating Streamer

As in still water, the floating streamer technique can be used to good effect on a river. It is best fished slightly upstream and allowed to drift down with the natural flow of the water, the rod occasionally giving a little twitch to motivate the wings, to give the lure the effect of a wounded or dying fish.

[17]

Additional Patterns

The following list of flies are of both types, the imitative and the attractor. Some are from the United States, but most are from both amateur and professional fly dressers in this country.

The ABU series of Optic Lures

These lures, supplied by the famous Swedish tackle firm are all adorned with bead eyes, and are extremely good lures for all species of game fish. The three main patterns each have three variations, namely a silver version, a black bodied version and an orange bodied version.

Before introducing these flies to the public they were rigorously tested on ABU's private lake Vitta Vatta, meaning 'White Water'. On this lake they more than proved themselves, for the lake is stocked with Rainbow, Brown Trout, Brook Trout, Arctic Char and Black Bass, records for the first two months of testing showed that the fish taken were caught nine times out of ten on these optic flies.

The names Call Girl, Playboy, Pin Up, and Streamtease, were inspired by a notorious scandal involving call girls etc. the original name for the 'Call Girl' was in fact the name of one of the two girls that made headlines at that time.

Call Girl

TAIL. Orange hackle fibres.

BODY. Flat silver tinsel, oval silver rib.

WING. Orange dyed squirrel tail and strands of bronze peacock.

HACKLE. Blue spotted guinea fowl.
HEAD. Black, silver bead eyes.

Playboy
TAIL. Orange hackle fibres.
BODY. Silver tinsel oval silver rib.
WING. Black squirrel, bronze peacock herl.
HACKLE. Orange cock hackle.
HEAD. Black, silver bead eyes.

Pin Up
TAIL. Scarlet hackle fibres.
BODY. Flat silver tinsel, oval tinsel rib.
WING. Natural squirrel, bronze peacock herl.
HACKLE. Bright blue cock.

Streamtease
TAIL. Golden pheasant tippet fibres.
BODY. Flat silver tinsel, oval tinsel rib.
WING. Squirrel and peacock herl.
HACKLE. Fiery brown.

As stated earlier, all four lures can have black/silver rib, orange/ silver rib bodies also. ABU's also sell tube fly versions of the same lures.

Tied Down Lures
By tied down lures I mean flies similar in construction to such flies as the Jersey Herd, the winging medium tied down at the tail end of the fly to form the back of the lure and also the fishlike tail.

Norris Shakespeare of Redditch, Worcs. supplies the following fly:

Tied Down Alexander
BODY. Flat silver tinsel oval silver rib.
HACKLE. Black beard hackle.

WING.   Green peacock herl, red ibis or dyed swan sides. Tied down head and tail.

The two following lures were conceived by Bob Worrell of The Angler's Corner, Croydon, Surrey, both are tied down lures and both have taken many good trout in the reservoirs of Southern England.

Tied Down Black Marabou (Worrell)
BODY.   Black floss silk, tapered oval silver rib.
WING.   Black marabou tied down head and tail.
HACKLE.   None.

Green and Black Bucktail (Worrell)
BODY.   Black floss silk tapered oval silver tinsel.
WING.   Black bucktail, green bucktail over, tied down head and tail.
HACKLE.   None.

David Train of Stratton St. Margaret, near Swindon, Wilts., whose multi-hook lures were given in the chapter on the same, sent me the following pattern called The Last Resort. This fly is an imitation of a Roach Fry.

The Last Resort (Train)
BODY.   White acetate floss silk, built into fish shape, treated with solvent and flattened at the sides. When dry the floss is then covered with flat silver lurex, then lapped with polythene strip (like Polystickle), at the head end of the fly two small tufts of magenta fluorescent floss either side to act as fins. The polythene is then ribbed with silver wire.
WING.   Twisted strands of bronze peacock herl and blue bucktail, tied down at tail.
HEAD.   Peacock herl (the Jungle cock flanks the head only).

A strip of white swan feather can be added as under belly, below the ribbing tinsel, but this is optional.

The following 'Foxtail Flies' were devised by Dr. Graham Priestly, an extremely competent fly dresser and excellent angler. He fished both flies successfullly at Weirwood reservoir.

Black Foxtail (Priestly)

TAIL. Golden pheasant tippet fibres.

BODY. Tapered white floss.

RIB. Alternate bands of silver wire and purple tying silk.

WING. Natural fox tail.

HACKLE. Beard hackle of black cock.

CHEEK. Tied very short at the head, two black and white guinea fowl feathers (Black/White).

HEAD. Black.

Orange Foxtail (Priestly)

As the above pattern but with a beard hackle of dyed orange cock.

The next perch type lure was sent to me by A. D. Bradbury of Altrincham, Cheshire. He has had many fish from Grafham Water. Mr. Bradbury also dresses many effective nymph and May fly patterns.

Adbury Streamer (Bradbury)

TAIL. Arc chrome DRF floss four strands.

BODY. Flat silver tinsel.

WING. Four grizzle hackles.

CHEEK. Jungle cock.

HACKLE. Orange cock hackle, beard fashion.

H. A. B. Clements, a professional fly dresser from Cossington, gave me the dressing of a grey wing lure that he tied for a customer which fishes very well at Grafham in September. As he couldn't furnish me with the name of the lure I shall refer to it as a 'Grey Wing'.

Grey Wing Streamer (Clements)

TAIL. None.

BODY.   Tapered black floss.
RIB.   None.
WING.   Two strips of grey duck feather back to back.
HACKLE.   None.
HEAD.   Bulky peacock herl.

The world renowned fishing tackle firm of C. Farlow & Co. Ltd. of Pall Mall have amongst their vast range of flies a series of Bucktail and Streamer flies devised by Richard Aylot. These flies have proved very successful early in the season on such waters as Grafham. Both streamers and the bucktails are of the 'flasher' type of lure.

Farlows Murderers
Silver

TAIL.   Lime fluorescent wool.
BODY.   Embossed silver tinsel.
WINGS.   Two grizzle hackles.
CHEEK.   Jungle cock.
HACKLE.   Yellow cock.

Black

TAIL.   Fluorescent red wool.
BODY.   Black floss.
RIB.   White fluorescent silk.
WINGS.   Two black cock hackles.
CHEEK.   Jungle cock.
HACKLE.   Dyed red cock.

Gold

TAIL.   Fluorescent red wool.
BODY.   Wide oval gold tinsel.
WING.   Two grizzle cock hackles.
CHEEK.   Jungle cock.
HACKLE.   Red cock.

In all cases the heads of the above flies are black and are available on long shank hooks sizes 4 to 8.

Farlows 'AA' Bucktail Lures
Red
- TAIL.   Fluorescent red wool.
- BODY.   Flat silver tinsel.
- RIB.   Oval silver tinsel.
- WING.   Dyed squirrel tail, red.
- HACKLE.   White.

Orange
- TAIL.   Fluorescent yellow wool.
- BODY.   Flat silver tinsel.
- RIB.   Oval silver tinsel.
- WING.   Dyed squirrel, hot orange.
- HACKLE.   White.

Yellow
- TAIL.   Fluorescent lime green wool.
- BODY.   Flat silver tinsel.
- RIB.   Oval silver tinsel.
- WING.   Dyed squirrel, yellow.
- HACKLE.   White.

Stephens Fishing Tackle of Stevenage, Herts., one of the country's leading suppliers of stillwater fly fishing tackle, market a wide selection of flies. Amongst these are a number of Streamer, Bucktail and Stickle type lures. Mr. R. D. Stephens kindly sent me the following dressings which have proved their worth on many of the large reservoirs such as Grafham and Chew Valley.

Stephens Stickle Flies
All the following patterns are based on the original Polystickle conception of Richard Walker.

Roach Fry Polystickle
- TAIL AND BACK.   Blue Raffene.
- BODY.   Wound polythene over bare gold hook that has a spiral of black tying silk to provide the rib of the fish, a little

red wool or silk at the head of the fly under the polythene imitates the fish's innards.

HACKLE.   Red scarlet throat hackle.
HEAD.   Black.

Lumistickle
TAIL AND BACK.   Lime green Raffene.
BODY.   Luminous plastic strip (Stephens market the same).
HACKLE.   Orange/Yellow bucktail, throat hackle.
HEAD.   Black.

Phantom Polystickle
TAIL AND BACK.   White Raffene.
BODY.   Polythene over white rayon floss.
HACKLE.   Lemon yellow throat hackle.
HEAD.   White, black eye.

Male Stickleback
TAIL AND BACK.   Dark green Raffene.
BODY.   Polythene wound over golden olive floss.
HACKLE.   Scarlet throat hackle.
HEAD.   White grey on top, red beneath and with black eye.

Female Stickleback
TAIL AND BACK.   Dark green Raffene.
BODY.   Polythene wound over white rayon floss.
HACKLE.   Teal throat hackle.
HEAD.   White, grey on top, grey beneath with black eye.

Stephens Mylar Bodied Flies
Mylar Olive
TAIL.   None.
BODY.   Silver mylar tubing.
HACKLE.   Short cock, dark scarlet almost magenta.
WING.   Yellowy olive bucktail.
HEAD.   Yellow, black eye.

Mylar Black

TAIL. None.
BODY. Silver mylar tubing.
HACKLE. Scarlet cock.
WING. Black bucktail.
HEAD. Black.

Mylar Texas Rose

TAIL. None.
BODY. Silver mylar tubing.
HACKLE. Orange cock hackle the length of body.
WING. Yellow bucktail.
HEAD. Yellow, black eye.

The next three flies from the Stephens stable are a Streamer, a Bucktail and, well I will leave the reader to judge the third of the trio. All have had their fair share of fish at Grafham.

White Featherwing

TAIL. None.
BODY. White floss silk.
RIB. Oval silver wire.
WING. Four white saddle hackles.
HEAD. White, black eyes.

Ashanti

TAIL Red wool.
BODY. Rear two thirds blue and silver lurex alternative bands, final third red DFM wool.
HACKLE. Scarlet.
WING. Black squirrel, red bucktail over.
HEAD. Black.

John Thomas

TAIL. Long tips of peacock herl from the eye part of the feather, about 12 strands.

BODY. Peacock herl (eye feather herl) wound over a floss underbody to give a tapered body.

Before the head a collar of red DFM wool is wound on.

HEAD. Black.

For their hooks Stephens Fishing tackle use gold plated Mustad 4XL 79581 and Mustad Bronze 7962.

The heads of some of Stephens lures are sometimes constructed out of clear monofil nylon, and tying silks are matched to the back or wing.

William Iveson of Brampton, Huntingdon dresses flies for all parts of the country for trout, salmon and seatrout, but living close to Grafham Water many of his flies are used on that reservoir. The following five flies he ties for customers who fish Grafham.

The first fly was suggested to the dresser by Mr. Reg Wayman of Huntingdon who has taken many good fish on it, one over four pounds in the 1970 season.

Jersey Herd Variant

BACK AND BODY. As for conventional herd.

WING. From a fox's pelt.

HACKLE. Orange collar.

HEAD. Bronze peacock herl.

Polystickle Variants (Iveson)

(1)

BODY. Wrapped polythene ribbed over with silver oval tinsel.

HACKLE. Yellow.

BACK AND TAIL. Fox pelt, tied down at head and tail, varnished across the back.

(2)

BODY. As (1) ribbed silver tinsel, then coated with stencil correcting fluid, this is a fluorescent red varnish.

HACKLE. Blue dun tied either side of the head.

BACK AND TAIL. As (1).

Orange Bodied Muddler (Iveson)
TAIL. None.
BODY. Orange seals fur well picked out.
WING. Badger under fur dyed yellow (this fur is effectively crinkly).
HEAD. As conventional muddler.

The following marabou fly is a killer on Grafham Water, on one occasion taking five prime fish in a three hour session.

Black Marabou (Iveson)
BODY. Tapered black floss silk (fairly bulky).
RIB. Oval silver tinsel.
HACKLE. Scarlet.
WING. Black marabou.

Further tandem lures from Tom C. Saville Ltd. These lures are in addition to the large selection mentioned in the chapter on multi-hook flies. There is not a company in this country to touch the firm of Saville's for quality and service, they often pioneer new flies and items of tackle, all of which are thoroughly tested and vetted before bringing to the notice of the angling public. So it is with these lures, all have caught their fair share of fish before appearing in their excellent catalogue.

Claret Lure (Savilles)
TAIL. Golden pheasant tippets.
BODY. Claret seals fur.
RIB. Gold oval rib.
Second Hook
BODY. As above.
HACKLE. Black cock beard.
WING. Brown bucktail.

Bloody Nora (Savilles)
TAIL. Red floss (DFM).
BODY. Embossed silver tinsel.

Second Hook
    BODY. As rear hook.
    HACKLE. Scarlet cock.
    WING. Black squirrel.

Stickleback Lure (Savilles)
    TAIL. Golden pheasant tippet fibres.
    BODY. Embossed silver tinsel.
Second Hook
    BODY. As rear hook.
    HACKLE. Scarlet cock.
    WING. Black bucktail over dark green bucktail.

White Mary Anne Lure (Savilles)
    TAIL. Red floss.
    BODY. White floss, silver rib.
Second Hook
    BODY. As rear hook.
    HACKLE. Blue hackle fibres.
    WING. White polar bear.
    CHEEK. Jungle cock.

Yellow and Black Lure (Savilles)
    TAIL. None.
    BODY. Black floss.
    RIB. Silver oval tinsel.
Front Hook
    BODY. Same as rear hook.
    HACKLE. Black cock fibres.
    WING. Red bucktail over yellow bucktail.

In John Veniard's book *Reservoir and Lake Flies* he gives three British streamer flies. The first two are tied by Roy Masters, then the third by Alec Iles. All are based on North American originals.

The Chief (Masters)
    TAG. Silver tinsel.

BODY. Fluorescent scarlet floss.

RIB. Oval silver tinsel.

WINGS. Two yellow hen hackles on the inside, two scarlet cock hackles on the outside.

CHEEK. Jungle cock cheeks.

HACKLE. Collar hackle mixed scarlet and yellow cock.

HEAD. Black.

The Cree (Masters)

TAIL. Light brown cock fibres.

BODY. Underbody of lead wire, silver lurex over.

WINGS. Two small cree hackles inside, two larger cree hackles outside.

CHEEK. Jungle cock.

HACKLE. Collar style long mixed yellow and scarlet cock hackles.

Breathaliser (Iles)

TAIL. Black cock hackle fibres.

BODY. Flat silver tinsel.

RIB. None.

WINGS. Two hot orange hackles inside, two green highlander hackles outside.

CHEEK. Jungle cock tied short.

HACKLE. Collar style badger.

In an earlier chapter I gave the dressing of an Orange Streamer, the following bucktail is a hair version, using orange as the basic colour. On this fly I have taken many good rainbow trout. Why the colour orange attracts rainbow trout I do not know, but it appears to.

Orange Bucktail (Price)

TAIL. None.

BODY. Even turns of No. 8 oval gold.

WING. Sparse orange bucktail.

HACKLE. None.

HEAD. Black, white eye, black pupil.

The first time I tried the Banded Squirrel Bucktail I caught fourteen brown trout in very short succession. Since that occasion it has proved its worth on such reservoirs as Hanningfield, where it has caught fish when other flies just did not tempt a single trout.

Banded Squirrel Bucktail (Price)

TAIL.   Bunch of grey squirrel fibres.
BODY.   Light mauve wool, silver or gold rib.
WING.   Grey squirrel, (white tip, black bar, brown root).
HACKLE.   White bucktail the length of body, short red hackle fibres at the throat.
HEAD.   Black.

Amongst the many patterns tied and sold by David Train are a series of single hook streamers and bucktail flies. All in turn have proved themselves on most reservoirs in the country. Mr. Train himself fishes Chew Valley and Blagdon, and the following lures are the medicine for the trout on those waters.

Jungle Grey (Train)

TAIL.   Fluorescent magenta wool.
BODY.   Flat gold tinsel, oval gold rib.
WING.   Grey squirrel.
CHEEK.   Jungle cock.
HACKLE.   Beard hackle grey hen.

Black Hairwing Terror (Train)

TAIL.   Fan of golden pheasant tippets.
BODY.   Silver tinsel oval silver rib.
WING.   Black squirrel, four strands of peacock sword over.
HACKLE.   Beard of scarlet hen.

Olive Hairwing Terror (Train)

As the above fly except the wing is of olive dyed squirrel.

Brown Squirrel Lure (Train)

TAIL.   Scarlet hen fibres.

BODY. Flat silver tinsel oval rib.
WING. Parey squirrel.
HACKLE. Beard of black hen.

Black Squirrel Lure (Train)
As above pattern but with black squirrel wing.

Black and Blue Lure (Train)
TAIL. None.
BODY. Black floss silk ribbed with wide silver tinsel and oval tinsel.
WING. Black squirrel.
CHEEK. Jungle cock.
HACKLE. Kingfisher blue beard hackle.

Grey Darta (Train)
TAIL. Fan of golden pheasant tippet strands.
BODY. Blue floss silk, ribbed wide flat tinsel, oval tinsel over the flat.
WING. Grey Mallard flank.
CHEEK. Jungle cock.
HACKLE. Fibres of grey mallard flank.
HEAD. White.

Black Darta (Train)
As above pattern but with a dyed black swan wing, and black head.

Olive Darta (Train)
As Grey Darta but with an olive dyed swan wing.

Pheasant Darta (Train)
TAIL. Arc chrome wool.
BODY. Silver tinsel ribbed oval silver wire.
WING. Hen pheasant centre tail.
HACKLE. Dyed blue guinea fowl.
HEAD. Black, white eye, red pupil.

Fluorescent Grey Squirrel (Train)

TAIL. Phosphor yellow fluorescent wool.

BODY. Silver tinsel oval tinsel rib.

WING. Grey squirrel.

CHEEK. Jungle cock.

HACKLE. Beard of black hen.

Fluorescent Orange Squirrel (Train)

TAIL. Phosphor yellow fluorescent wool.

BODY. Flat gold tinsel ribbed oval gold tinsel.

WING. Orange dyed squirrel tail.

CHEEK. Jungle cock.

HACKLE. Beard of orange hen.

Fluorescent Hairwing Badger

TAIL. None.

BODY. Black floss.

RIB. Wide silver tinsel ribbed oval tinsel.

HACKLE. Fluorescent magenta hackle.

WING. White bucktail, black bucktail over, then white over that.

HEAD. Black, white eye, black pupil.

Red and White Lure

TAIL. None.

TAG. Flat silver tinsel.

BODY. Red wool.

RIB. Flat silver tinsel, ribbed narrow oval tinsel.

HACKLE. White cock.

WING. White bucktail, two strips of scarlet dyed swan.

Often the most simple of bucktail flies are the most successful, especially for catching the discriminating brown trout. The following six bucktails, though simple in design and colour can be killer patterns on their day.

Black and Silver Bucktail

TAIL. Scarlet swan.

BODY. Flat silver tinsel.
RIB. Oval silver rib.
WING. Black bucktail.
HEAD. Black (black pupil eye optional).

Black and White Bucktail
As above pattern but with the wing comprising black bucktail above white bucktail in equal proportion.

Black and Yellow Bucktail
As above but as the name suggests black over yellow bucktail.

Red and Yellow Bucktail
As above with red bucktail over yellow, the addition of a further band of yellow bucktail yields the Mickey Finn.

Red and White Bucktail
As above with red over white bucktail wing.

Grey Squirrel and Silver
TAIL. None.
BODY. Flat silver tinsel, oval rib.
WING. Grey squirrel.
HACKLE. None.

Painted eyes can be added to all these flies should the dresser favour this particular form of adornment.

The old and well tried British trout fly The Coachman, which was ostensibly tied to represent a small moth, crossed the Atlantic, there it took the guise of Royalty in the now equally well known Royal Coachman. Both patterns underwent a remarkable transformation in both the dry Fan Wing form, and also in the elongated flies we are concerned with in this book.

The Coachman Streamer
TAIL. None.

L

BODY.   Bronze peacock herl.

WING.   Two long slips of white swan or goose extending beyond the bend of the hook.

CHEEK.   Jungle cock (optional).

HACKLE.   Brown hen.

The Black or Dark Coachman Streamer.

As above pattern but with a body of black chenille or black dyed ostrich herl.

Royal Coachman Streamer

TAIL.   Golden pheasant tippets.

BODY.   In three parts Peacock herl/Red floss/Peacock herl.

WING.   Four white saddle hackles.

CHEEK.   Jungle cock.

HACKLE.   Brown hen.

The wings of both coachman flies can be varied with white bucktail or white marabou.

Judging from their appearance in most American catalogues it must be true to say that the coachman type of fly is still one of the most popular patterns on both sides of the Atlantic.

Another pattern, the dressing for which was kindly sent to me by Dan Gapen of the Gapen Fly Co. Inc. of Anoka, Minnesota, is the Skykomish Sunrise Streamer. I liked the poetic sound of this fly. It is also tied as a bucktail fly.

Skykomish Sunrise Streamer

TAIL.   Two strips of dyed red and yellow swan.

BODY.   Red floss, silver rib.

WING.   White cock hackles.

HACKLE.   Mixed red and yellow collar.

A well known North American trout fly is the basis for a very popular streamer or bucktail, the Parmachene Belle.

Parmachene Belle

TAIL.   Red and yellow swan slips or small bunches of bucktail of like colour.
BODY.   Yellow floss silk.
RIB.   Flat gold tinsel.
WING.   White bucktail over thin band of red bucktail over white bucktail.
HACKLE.   Mixed white and yellow hackle fibres.

A built wing of dyed and white swan can be substituted and a collar hackle used.

Palmered streamer flies have been dealt with under the heading of 'Dry Flies'. However a very provocative series of lures can be evolved for wet fly/lure fishing by using the same principle but utilising a long fibred soft hackle insead of the stiff cock hackle used for the dry streamers. A streamer or bucktail lure tied with a soft long fibred hen hackle as a body will yield a lure that can be fished very slowly but still have in its integral makeup an overall pulsating movement that can prove irresistible to predatory fish. The following dressing is just one example of many that can be evolved using the same basic design, a design that to my mind has been neglected for too long.

Palmered Black Lure

TAIL.   Red floss or wool.
BODY.   Heavily palmered black hen or soft cock hackle.
WING.   Black cock hackles back to back.
CHEEK.   Jungle cock.

Another 'Palmered' streamer of American origin is the White Miller. This is based on a conventional trout fly of the same name. This fly is not only used for all species of trout but is considered a good streamer pattern for Small Mouthed Bass.

The White Miller

TAIL.   Two white hackle tips back to back.

BODY. Palmered white hackle.

WING. Two white hackles back to back or white bucktail.

HEAD. Black with painted eye.

The Parmachene Belle, the dressing for which has already been given in this chapter, also appears as a palmered fly, again a fly favoured for the many panfish of the U.S.A. Flies of this palmered nature may well prove killing for our Pike as they have both mobility and bulk that is necessary in lures designed to take the largest of our predatory fish.

The Palmered Parmachene

TAIL. Red and white hackle fibres.

BUTT. Red chenille.

BODY. White or yellow chenille.

BODY HACKLE. White cock (sometimes a mixture of red and white).

WING. White then red then white bucktail.

HEAD. Black (sometimes painted with an eye with red pupil).

Once more I am indebted to John Veniard for the following four North American streamer patterns.

The Sandborn Streamer

TAG. Flat gold tinsel.

BODY. Black floss silk.

RIB. Flat gold tinsel.

HACKLE. Beard hackle of yellow cock fibres.

WING. Four yellow cock hackles.

CHEEK. Jungle cock.

HEAD. Black.

Examples of Black Marabou flies have already been given, the following Mylar bodied fly is another, on this occasion using white marabou. This is based on an American pattern.

White Marabou

BODY. Silver mylar (silver Goldfingering).

HACKLE. Scarlet cock fibres.
WING. White marabou, green peacock over.
CHEEK. Jungle cock.
HEAD. Black.

The following two bucktail flies are amongst the most popular in North America for most species of game fish.

Edson Light Tiger
TAIL. Barred wood duck.
BODY. Silver tip, the remainder bronze peacock herl.
WING. Yellow bucktail, short red hackle point on top.
CHEEKS. Close to the head short jungle cock.

Edson Dark Tiger
TAIL. Barred wood duck.
BODY. Yellow chenille with a silver tip.
HACKLE. Scarlet hackle spike at the throat tied very short.
WING. Brown bucktail, peacock herl over.
CHEEKS. Short jungle cock close to head.

The Spruce is a Western States fly, sometimes thought to represent small fingerling trout, others are of the opinion that it is a representation of a Bullhead/Sculpin type minnow with a broad head. A modern deerhair fly called the Spuddler has been evolved from the combination of the Spruce Streamer and a Muddler type of fly.

The Spruce
TAIL. Three or four green peacock herls $\frac{5}{8}$ in long.
BODY. Tail end about one-third floss silk, the remainder bulky bronze peacock herl.
WING. Four badger hackles.
HACKLE. Collar hackle of badger.

Throughout 1970 Tom Saville and his colleagues have been testing a new lure, the Saville version of the Spuddler, this will be

L*

available for the 1971 season as it proved to be highly attractive to both species of trout. The dressing is as follows:

Saville's Spuddler
TAIL.   Dark brown calf tail, bison or brown bear hair.
BODY.   Cream wool or fur with a few turns of scarlet fluorescent wool to suggest gill coloration.
WINGS. Dyed brown well marked grizzle hackles back to back.
COLLAR. (Hackle). Above hook only Canadian fox squirrel tail.
HEAD.   Dark deer hair clipped into flat tadpole shape.

The following simple bucktail fly from New Zealand has proved effective for both brown and rainbow trout in this country. In larger sizes it can be a very useful sea lure.

The Blondie (New Zealand)
TAIL.   Long bunch of white mohair cut off flat.
BODY.   Flat silver tinsel.
WING.   White mohair as long as the end of the tail and cut. off flush with it.

White bucktail or goathair can be substituted for the mohair.

Red and Black Matuka (New Zealand)
TAIL.   None.
BODY.   Red chenille.
RIB.   Oval gold tinsel.
WING.   Black hen hackles (tied down along the back with the ribbing medium).

One of the good things about the animal the Ringcat is the fact that it possesses a long barred black and white tail. By using the black hair as a wing and the white hair as the under body a whole series of Ringcat flies can be created. I have found this fly very successful when a small bucktail is desired, so I normally tie this series of flies on size 14 long shank fine wire hooks. The only factor that changes in the pattern is of course the body, the wing is always black and the underbody always white.

Ringcat and Silver
Flat silver tinsel, oval rib.

Ringcat and Gold
Flat gold tinsel, oval gold rib.

Ringcat and Black
Black floss, silver wire rib.

Ringcat and Orange
Orange floss and gold rib.

I have found the above four most successful, however the fly dresser can run through the whole spectrum if so desired.

[18]

Streamers and Bucktails for Coarse Fish

Pike

The use of flies for pike is well known and it is a most satisfying method of catching these freshwater sharks. Flies have been used for this fish for a good number of years. In a book published in the nineteenth century called the Scientific Angler by D. Foster, he quotes the use of large flies being used on the Shannon. An interesting fact about the traditional fly which he describes is the fact that the fly was adorned with bead eyes, one of the first optic streamers. The dressing given was similar to the dressing given by that famous angler John Bickerdyke in his book *The All Round Angler*, published at the end of the last century. The author theorises that the Pike fly is taken for a bird. A Book of Angling by Francis Francis published I believe in the 1860s also gives the same dressing. It is probable that they all cribbed from each other or from an earlier source. The dressing is as follows:

The Pike Fly
Large Double Hook

    TAIL.   Coloured hackles.

    BODY.   As thick as a little finger and of dyed pigs wool, blue yellow and green, ribbed with wide gold tinsel.

    HACKLES.   Heron hackle (Palmered).

    WING.   Peacock eye feathers.

    HEAD.   Two glass bead eyes.

Apparently this fly can be varied with peacock sword wings, and with pheasant hackles.

A short while ago I took great pleasure in reading of an American angler fishing for pike, noticing a small squirrel swimming across the river, then being engulfed in the huge ferocious maw of a large pike. The angler in question tied a large bucktail surface lure and subsequently caught the monster. Bickerdyke mentions in his book of an Irish method that employs the end of a calf's tail, again fished on the surface representing a rat. If these facts do not do anything else they prove there is very little new.

Why more pike anglers have not developed a fly fishing facet to their repertoire I do not know. They seem content to hurl into the water large spinners and progressively larger plugs, live bait and smelly herrings in an effort to take these fish, and ignore completely the streamer, bucktail and tandem lure. Over the past two years there have appeared one or two articles on fly fishing for pike in the angling press, but too few to start a serious new cult.

Flies for pike must out of necessity be quite large and bulky, giving the fish a tempting mouthful. I use size 4 and 6 longshank and occasionally an extra longshank 2 made by Mustad.

Most patterns given in this book for trout and salmon and even for sea fish will in their turn on occasions take pike. The magical Muddler Minnow has accounted for many pike, especially when fished with a fast retrieve in the surface film.

The pike will feed at most depths right up to the surface. Vanishing ducklings bear witness to this, one minute swimming behind their mother, next pulled below the surface by some large pike. How many times have we read such accounts. Swimming voles and other terrestrial creatures caught out of their natural element fall victim to the cunning fish. It is not unknown for grass snakes when taking an occasional swim as is their wont, to vanish before your eyes.

There is a very wide scope in experimentation in lure design and extra patterns for taking pike. Lures to represent small ducklings and voles are quite within the capabilities of most fly tyers.

Regarding patterns for pike, larger sizes of many existing streamers will suffice, even the more gaudy of our traditional salmon flies will take fish. The following dressings are but a few which can be created for the express purpose of luring the pike. In dressing lures for pike the following points may well be worth bearing in mind.

1. Size   Longshank 4, 2 or tandem combination.
2. Bulk   Heavily dressed bodies of wool and chenille.
3. Flash   Wide silver ribbing or mylar cheeks an advantage.
4. Action   Lots of pulsating movement in the feathered or hair wings.
5. Colour   Bright colours such as reds, yellows, whites etc. (A look at the better fish taking metallic lures for colour can be a guide.)

Conventional fly fishing techniques can be used. One point to bear in mind is the make up of the leader, a heavy shock tip is advisable, a 35 lb point is not an exaggeration where large fish are to be anticipated. I have found a leader of the following make up in monofilament nylon to be as good as any, 3 ft 45 lbs/3 ft 35 lbs/ 2 ft 25 lbs/1½ ft 15 lbs/1 ft 10 lbs/then a point of 1 ft 20 lbs, or if the fish are known to be heavy the same length but of about 35 lbs. This leader not only presents the fly which out of necessity is large, but can withstand the power of the pike's attack.

The 'fly' can also be presented on conventional fixed spool tackle by means of a bubble type float.

A spinner fly combination can also be an effective method of taking good pike, the forward spinner providing flash, and the trailing feathered lure the attractive pulsating movement.

Dressings
The following list of patterns are suggested colour combinations that should prove attractive to the pike.

Red and White
    TAIL.   Red hackle fibres or two hackle points.
    BODY.   Heavy white chenille.
    RIB.   Wide silver tinsel.
    WING.   Two red hackles two white hackles, long and mobile, not tied back to back.
    HACKLE.   Mixed red and white collar hackle.

Black and White

TAIL.   Red hackle fibres, hackle points or even a tuft of scarlet wool.

BODY.   Heavy black chenille.

RIB.   Wide silver tinsel.

WING.   Black and white hackles tied as above pattern.

HACKLE.   Mixed black and white collar.

Red and Yellow

TAIL.   As above two patterns.

BODY.   Red chenille.

RIB.   Wide tinsel.

WING.   Red and yellow hackles tied as above pattern.

HACKLE.   Mixed red and yellow collar.

Wool can be substituted for the chenille in any of the above patterns, painted or bead eyes can be added if so desired.

Mylar Marabou Streamer

TAIL.   None.

BODY.   Silver tinsel ribbed oval silver tinsel.

WING.   Green marabou over white marabou.

CHEEK.   Broad strips of silver mylar.

HACKLE.   Underbody of white marabou and a spike of red cock hackle at the throat.

Virtually any colour combination can be utilised, what will succeed one day may fail miserably on another occasion, this is seen with plugs and spinners. Fish can be as fickle as women.

Fig. 39   Pike Lure

The following dressings are a combination of the muddler deer hair flies and the multi wing type of fly. Giving the lure a deer hair allows you to fish the lure almost as a floating plug. On retrieving this type of lure it has a tendency to dive, and resurface when the retrieve is stopped. This is due to the buoyant qualities of the deer hair.

Grizzle and Red

TAIL. None.

BODY. White chenille.

RIB. Silver tinsel rib.

WING. Two grizzle hackles, two red hackles.

HEAD AND COLLAR. Large broad head of clipped deer hair, a large proportion left unclipped to provide a collar.

EYES. Two optic beads, (these beads are tied in during the spinning of the deer hair, the spinning is then continued until the head is complete, then clipped exposing the eyes).

Canary

TAIL. None.

BODY. White chenille.

RIB. Gold tinsel.

WING. Four yellow saddle hackles.

HEAD AND COLLAR. Clipped deer hair as last pattern.

EYES. Optic beads.

Grizzle and Silver

TAIL. None.

BODY. Flat silver tinsel, oval silver rib.

WING. Four long mobile grizzle hackles.

HEAD AND COLLAR. Deer hair as last pattern.

EYES. Optic beads.

Black Beasty

TAIL. None.

BODY. Black chenille.

WING. Four black saddle hackles.

HEAD.   Clipped deer hair as above pattern.
EYES.   Optic beads.

As with the first group of patterns, these latter flies can of course be varied giving the fly dresser a wide scope of colour combination.

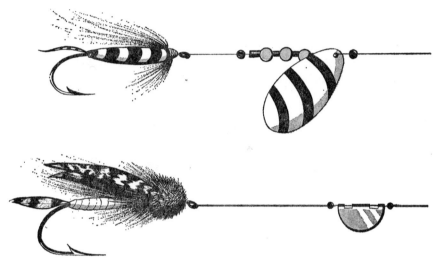

Fig. 40   Spinner Fly Combination

In the United States a whole range of 'deer hair' bugs are tied as surface lures for black bass and large trout. Such flies, like the frog discussed earlier can be used quite successfully for surface taking pike. One such fly sent to me by the Keel Hook Fly Company is the Gray Mouse. A lure used for both bass and trout should also have some attraction for our pike. This pattern of course makes use of the Keel Hook and a deer hair head like the last group of flies. The illustration will show exactly the appearance of this rather bizarre mouse. Fig. 41.

Gray Mouse (Keel Fly Co.)
   TAIL.   Deer hair and two scarlet hackle tips and two grizzle hackle tips, these hackles are as long as the body of the fly.

BODY. This is comprised of the hackles and the deer hair, both are tied on near the head of the fly and are whipped on to the hook shank, leaving the hair end and the hackle points as the tail.

HACKLE. Long grizzle collar.

WING. Unclipped deer body hair.

HEAD. Flat wedge shape of clipped deer hair.

One of the best methods of attracting pike is to fish both the surface and subsurface lures with a fairly slow retrieve, then nearing the end of the retrieve to accelerate the fly. This sudden change of speed often prompts the following pike to seize the lure, in fear

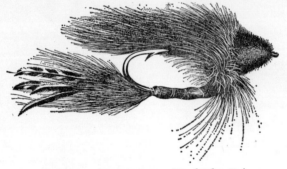

Fig. 41   Gray Mouse (Keel Fly Co)

that it is about to lose it. Always fish the cast right out, pike will follow the fly for quite some time before taking, often coming right into the bank before attacking.

Perch

I think it is true to say that in all probability the record for this fish could well be broken by an angler fishing for trout on one of the modern reservoirs. Many large perch thrive in such waters, but what will be more significant is the fact that the fish will be taken on an artificial fly using conventional fly fishing techniques.

Let's face it, it can be only too easy to catch this hungry and seemingly greedy fish when we are after the more regal trout. Catches of 50 or 60 small perch can occur on some waters. There are a few entries in my fishing diary that read 'One brown trout, one rainbow, and 40 small perch to 1 lb'. These fish seem to roam the waters in seemingly endless shoals forcing the trout angler to pick up his bag and move to fresh areas.

The perch that we desire is the larger more solitary tiger striped denizen, whose stripes camouflage him between the reed stalks and the olive deeps. Methods of fly fishing for perch should not vary from methods evolved for other species of fly caught fish. The fact that we can catch so many during a trout fishing sortie is proof of this. However the angler will stand a better chance of catching large perch if he uses a fly approximating the perch's natural prey, minnow type flies or the representation of roach, perch and other fry.

I remember thinking that this minnow type fly was the answer to better than the run of the mill perch, having taken one or two good fish using this type of lure. The next day I took equally good perch on a small wet Greenwells Glory. But I do not think that this alters the fact that the big perch is going to fall to a streamer or bucktail lure.

Sizes of fly between longshank 8 to longshank 4 I think would be about right for large perch. Regarding patterns, the following are but a few of the many that will suffice.

Polystickle types.
Herds.
Minnow streamers.
Roach and Perch fry streamers and bucktails.

Any fly spinner combination too will prove effective on such waters that will allow this method.

In the United States they have a greater variety of fly taking fish. Many of the 'Pan Fish', that is what they call them, are similar in feeding habits to our own perch, feeding on worms crustacea and small fish. The following lure patterns tied on light wire long shank hooks are considered fine fare for the Blue Gill, Yellow Perch and Rock Bass etc. they may well prove of equal attraction for our striped denizen. Size of hook size 12 to size 14 in all cases.

Bream Streamer

TAIL.   Yellow cock hackle fibres.
BODY.   Black floss silk.
RIB.   Oval silver tinsel.
HACKLE.   Yellow spike hackle.
WING.   White bucktail or any white hair.

Fig. 42   Delta Queen

Delta Queen

TAIL.   Teal feather (American pattern calls for barred wood duck).
BODY.   White floss silk.
RIB.   Flat gold tinsel.
HACKLE.   Yellow spike hackle.
WING.   Light tan hair (Bucktail or mink).
CHEEK.   Jungle cock.

Minnow Mite

TAIL.   Grizzle hackle fibres.
BODY.   Mole fur or dubbed grey wool.
HACKLE.   Spike hackle ginger or light natural red.
WING.   Grey bucktail or any grey hair.
HEAD.   Black and white bead or painted white eye, black pupil.

Deep White

TAIL.   None.
BODY.   Flat silver tinsel, silver rib (optional).
HACKLE.   White collar hackle.
WING.   Two long splayed out hackles.
HEAD.   White head, yellow eye, red pupil.

Other Coarse Fish

Having dealt with the Pike and Perch, the truly pisciverous of our coarse fish, we are left with a number of fish that are both herbivorous and insectivorous. But there are times when these fish forget their usual diet and will take small fish. I feel it will not be long before that introduced fish the Zander will be sought for with artificial lures rather than with the present lobworm baits.

Chub

I would put the white mouthed chub next on the list of fish that will not say no to a properly presented lure. Most flies given in books for chub are dry insect representations of a conventional dressing, i.e. Black Gnat, or the heavily palmered dry flies. The 'dry' streamers and bucktails given in the earlier chapter can prove on occasions excellent chub catching flies.

Small Muddlers, Hoppers and Stoneflies—all will take the shy, shadowy chub. As for subsurface flies, flies tied to represent minnow etc. will in all probability prove just as effective.

Let us be fair, a real minnow will take far more chub than any artificial minnow, but one of the main reasons why we do not hear of large chub being taken on streamers or bucktails is simply because not many people seek the chevender with such lures, it is as simple as that.

Dace

The silver dace is a noted fly taker. However the smaller conventional dry flies would be the right medicine rather than the larger lures, but this does not rule out the possibility of taking good sized dace on a streamer or bucktail.

Grayling

In my opinion the best flies to use for this 'Lady of the Rivers' are small insect type flies fished wet or dry. However there is a case for further experimentation in using larger flies, for this fish is often taken on bright spinners. This being the case there is no earthly reason why a fish simulating lure should not prove successful on occasions.

Roach and Rudd

In Europe, especially the Netherlands, it is quite common to fish for this family with large flies, spinners or spin/fly combinations.

Reservoir anglers whilst fishing for the more edible trout often connect with these silver and red beauties, sometimes of specimen proportions, 2 lbs or more. My best roach pulled down the scales at 2½ lbs. This was caught on a size 8 longshank. Too many roach have fallen to a streamer or bucktail lure for it to be a fluke, especially in the light of continental methods.

The Barbel

There are very few freshwater fish that can put up a fight like the barbel. The dogged power in the struggle even outpowers the salmon. In Germany the barbell is taken by means of streamer and bucktail flies. The largest taken on a fly tipped the scales at 10 lbs. What can be done in Germany surely can apply to this country too. We seem content to fish for this magnificent creature with the contents of our larder, sausage being one bait highly recommended, or with maggots and worms. There is a misconception in this country that any fish other than the game fish caught on a fly is a bit of a fluke. The more anglers that resort to using a fly, the more barbel will be taken. A Muddler Minnow or the like trotted down into the barbel lie may well produce a fish. This particular fly is a usual one to use in Germany.

There have been greater revolutions in angling than using flies for barbel, so instead of mucking up your hands with smelly sticky baits, give a large fly a chance.

What of carp and tench? I have seen accounts of both fish taken on nymph flies, but my researches have not thrown up any evidence of either fish falling to the allure of a streamer or bucktail fly. This doesn't mean to say it couldn't or wouldn't happen.

I am of the opinion that the shoaling bream can be taken on well sunk flies, but the flies that would tempt them, would be small larva imitating flies rather than the larger lures mentioned in this book. There have, however been a few accounts of this fish falling to a spinner, so you can never really tell.

[19]

Sea Fishing Lures

There is nothing new in seeking saltwater fish by means of feathered lures. Many a young angler, and some not so young, start their fishing pastime by feathering for the shoals of summer mackerel. Throughout the world many species of fish are sought by fish simulating lures made of feathers. To this day some commercial fishermen seek the Tunny or Tuna with a large feathered lure. When small tunny are sighted they are encouraged by chumming—the throwing overboard of bucketfuls of small fish and guts etc., what we in this country term as rubby dubby. The fisherman uses a single pole and a fixed line and jigs the lure in the water. On striking the fish he heaves the fish overhead, the lure has a barbless hook and the tunny falls behind him, and he continues to catch fish whilst the craze for feeding is still on them. When larger tunny fish are accounted two men with two poles and a single line tackle the larger tunny fishing in concert. When the very large fish are on the scene three men and three poles connected to one line fish for these giant fish. In all cases they use feathered lures and barbless hooks. Some of the fish sought by game fishermen throughout the world by means of flies are as follows: Species of Marlin, the Tarpon, an overgrown Herring which can reach in excess of 200 lbs. Bonefish, Barracuda, King Mackerel, Amberjack, Jewfish, Sailfish, Channel Bass etc., etc., the list is endless.

Around British waters a number of fish are regularly caught by the same means, mackerel, garfish, coalfish, bass, cod, ling, pollack, whiting, even the winter herring. But with a lot of thought, patience and with the right type of feathered lure, sharks, tope, perhaps even halibut may well be taken in our waters.

The three methods of using feathered lures for sea fishing are:

1. Conventional fly fishing.
2. Trolling.
3. Jigging.

Conventional fly fishing can be conducted from shores into surf for bass, utilising shooting head type lines, from rocky promontories into deeper water, to dimpling bass or seatrout or from a slow moving or static boat.

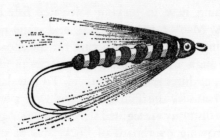

Fig. 43   Bass Lure

The second method must of course be carried out from an oar propelled or powered boat, the lure either trailing behind on the surface skipping enticingly in the water, or the lure by means of weights is trolled along the sea bed.

The third method of using feathered lures is by jigging. The lure is lowered into the water, the bottom found, the lure lifted up a few feet, and by moving the rod in a tight 6 in to 1 ft arc the lure is activated. This jigging method can be carried out from either boats, or from piers and jetties.

In the past years salmon and seatrout flies were used successfully for Bass and other free feeding predators. Such patterns as the Goldfinch and Alexandra are mentioned in John Bickerdyke's *The All Round Angler.*

For methods of fishing with lures the reader would do well to read *Feathering for Sea Fish* by F. W. Holiday (Herbert Jenkins), or *Spinning and Trolling for Sea Fish* by Hugh Stoker (A. C. Black).

As our lure is supposed to be representing some sort of bait fish it is best represented by a longshank hook rather than a short shank, except in such lures that in their make up have extra long hair wings, and which utilise short shank hooks. There is also a case for the tandem fly, especially when we are trying to imitate larger baitfish for some of the sea's big fish.

The simplest form of feathered lure is the single white feather tied on to a bare hook, a seagull's feather or the like. This rough and ready lure tied as a matter of expediency has proved more than attractive for both bass and mackerel.

The Mackerel Feathers
SIZE.   Whiting hooks not too large.

Three or four saddle hackles of divers colours whipped to the head. There is no body dressing. Normally fished six to a trace.

Cod Feathers
As the Mackerel Feathers but on stronger hook. Quite often white saddle hackles only are used.

The Bodied Mackerel
This lure can have a variety of body colours made of wool and ribbed with wide silver tinsel.
TAIL.   None.
BODY.   Wool, i.e. red, white, etc.
WING.   Three coloured or saddle hackles, including white.

The small coalfish are often called Billett or Cuddies. The following fly is a traditional pattern used for Pollack.

The Cuddy Fly
TAIL.   Red.
BODY.   White wool.
RIB.   Flat gold tinsel.
WING.   Whole white or grey feather (goose, duck or seagull were used).

The modern fly dresser can of course utilise white goat hair or white hackles back to back to achieve greater mobility in the wing.

One of the historical sea flies for bass was called the Shaldon Shiner, the original dressing, according to Bickerdyke was as follows:

The Shaldon Shiner

TAIL.   Red feathers.

BODY.   Flat silver tinsel, green, red and blue pigswool at the shoulder.

WING.   Bright blue feathers, sometimes some grey moose fibres were added.

The modern dresser can of course substitute seal's fur for the older pigs wool, and saddle hackles dyed blue for the wing. For the soft mouthed Mullett of the estuaries our great grandfathers used a Mullett Fly fished at dusk or night. Occasionally the fly was baited with available shellfish.

The Mullett Fly

TAIL.   None.

BODY.   White wool silver tinsel over.

HACKLE.   White hen.

WING.   Mottled owl feather.

Another fly mentioned by Bickerdyke as being successful on occasions for the bass in the last century.

TAIL.   Long red hackle fibres.

BODY.   Thin red pigswool (seal fur as substitute).

HACKLE.   As tail.

WING.   Golden pheasant tail slips.

CHEEK.   Jungle cock.

Bickerdyke's Alexandra variants for bass, mackerel, coalfish and pollack, the original flies were in all probability tied on conventional shanked hooks, but the master suggests flies over an inch long. This being so they should fit into the streamer concept

by using longshank hooks. The Alexandra Streamer, the dressing
for which was given in an earlier chapter can also be tried out.

Grey Winged Alexandra
Long shank 4, 6
>   TAIL.   Green peacock herl and scarlet dyed goose fibres.
>   BODY.   Flat silver tinsel, silver wire rib.
>   HACKLE.   Black hen or few fibres of peacock herl (sword
>   feather).
>   WING.   Green peacock sword feather flanked either side by
>   strips of grey goose wing.

White Wing Alexandra
As above pattern but with white goose or swan instead of grey.

Red and White Alexandra
As above pattern but with white and scarlet goose flanking the
green herl.

All these old patterns caught their share of fish in their day, and
there is no reason why they should not do the same for the modern
angler.

The following patterns are amongst some that appeared in *A
Further Guide to Fly Dressing* by John Veniard, all are streamer flies.

1. BODY.   White chenille.
>   HACKLE.   Red collar hackle.
>   WING.   Six white saddle hackles.
>   HEAD.   White with black pupil eye.
2. BODY.   Flat silver tinsel.
>   HACKLE.   None.
>   WING.   Two scarlet dyed goose shoulder feathers back to
>   back.
>   HEAD.   Black, yellow eye, black pupil.
3. TAIL.   Red and white goose feathers.
>   BODY.   Embossed silver tinsel.
>   WING.   White marabou feathers.
>   CHEEK.   Red hackle tips, jungle cock over.
>   HEAD.   Black.

4. BODY. White chenille.
   HACKLE. White collar hackle.
   WING. Three white and three blue hackles.
   HEAD. Black.

In the book *World of Fishing* by Joe Brooks published in the U.S.A. by Van Nostrand, a book incidentally which will show what can be done by using flies, the fishing described therein will make your mouth water. Joe Brooks favours a group of flies called the 'Blondes', he used this type of fly for both trout fishing and seafishing for such species as small Tarpon. The famous company of Orvis tie their Blonde flies for seafishing on weedless hooks. There is a similarity between these flies and the New Zealand 'Blondie'.

Platinum Blonde (Brookes)

TAIL. White bucktail or polar bear.
BODY. Silver tinsel, ribbed silver oval (use non tarnishable tinsels for sea fishing).
WING. As tail.
HEAD. White.

On keel hooks the wing hair masks the hook point.

Honey Blonde (Brookes)

TAIL. Yellow bucktail or polar bear.
BODY. Silver tinsel, silver rib.
WING. Yellow bucktail as tail.
HEAD. White or yellow.

There are other colour combinations and single colour flies in Joe Brooke's series, and the dresser of course can create his own, it is again a question of a simple fly being an effective one.

It may well be that in future years sea fishing may well have a range of well tried and named patterns, like the vast range of well known flies for fresh water angling. In the United States this has already happened, but over here the sea angler who seeks his quarry with a feathered or fur lure is considered a bit strange to say the

least. Lures tied to represent the small fish that the predators feed on will obviously prove the more successful. The following suggested dressings are aimed at copying some of the small bait fish that abound around our coasts.

One of the finest baits for bass is the sandeel. I consider this little fish best represented by a tandem rigged three hook streamer.

The Sandeel Streamer

BODIES.   All three hooks flat silver tinsel ribbed oval tinsel.

WING.   Very long green saddle hackles (olive) white hackles below.

HEAD.   Green, white eye, black pupil.

Fig. 44   Sandeel Tandem Lure.

There can be more than one way of representing the young herring, the Brit. The following two will give the dresser some idea, and perhaps encourage him to improve on the same.

Marabou Brit

TAIL.   None.

BODY.   Heavy body of white wool, fluorescent wool is an advantage.

WING.   White marabou with green marabou over.

CHEEKS.   Strips of silver mylar.

HEAD.   White with red pupilled eye.

Streamer Brit

TAIL.   White hackle clipped to fishtail shape.

BODY.   Flat silver tinsel (mylar tubing can be used).

WING.   Two white saddle hackles.

SHOULDER.   Lady Amhurst tippets.

CHEEK.   Jungle cock.

UNDERBODY.   Two hackles as for wing.

M

In the section devoted to salmon patterns mention was made of the Elver Fly. The following dressing utilises more readily available feathers, as the Vulturine Galena used in the salmon lure is pretty scarce.

The Elver Streamer
BODY. Black silk.
RIB. Silver oval.
HACKLE. None.
WING. Two black or very dark blue hackles back to back, two badger hackles either side. Long slim saddle hackles preferred.
HEAD. Black.

Some of the larger bait fish are best imitated by means of two hooks in tandem. During the cold months of winter shoals of silvery sprats provide the large cod with a vast larder. The following lure is dressed with these sprats in mind.

Sprat Streamer Lure
Two hooks joined by a heavy wire linkage. Size of hook 2/0. The length of fly to be around 5 in or 6 in.
BODY. Both hooks white DFM wool.
WING. White marabou, pale blue marabou over, green marabou over all.
UNDERBODY. White marabou.
CHEEK. ⅜ in strip of silver mylar.
HACKLE. Front hook only, collar of scarlet cock.
HEAD. Olive green, then a painted red circle, white eye with black pupil.

The mackerel too can be represented by the same type of lure. It will not be long before sea anglers will seek the shark and like fish that feed on the mackerel, they will I feel sure use lures of this nature.

Mackerel Streamer Lure

Two hook rig heavy wire or nylon linkage. Size of hook from 2/0 to 4/0 depending on species sought. Size of fly 6 in to 10 in.

BODIES. White wool.

WING. Green and blue saddle hackles (on larger flies the wing is tied on both hooks to achieve length).

UNDER WING. White saddle hackles.

CHEEK. Broad strip of silver mylar, marked in vertical stripes, blue or green, by means of waterproof felt-tipped pen.

HACKLE. Long fibred collar hackle of white cock.

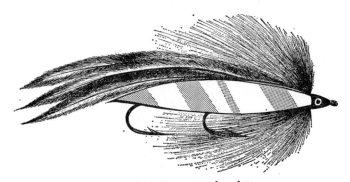

Fig. 45   Big Game Mackerel Lure

Shrimps and prawns also can be imitated in much the same way as the crayfish mentioned earlier. The use of fluorescent materials in the make up of all lures often enhances the fly and its fish catching potential increases.

A simple bass fly that I have been told is used in Ireland uses goat hair as the winging medium. I think the fly is all the better for a painted eye.

Goat Hair Bass Fly

TAIL. None.

BODY. Either white wool or red wool dressed heavily.

RIB. Wide silver tinsel.

WING. White goat hair extending beyond the tail.

UNDER WING. Same as wing.

HEAD. Black, white eye, black pupil.

The Squid and Cuttle Jig Streamer

Squid and cuttle fish around our coast also figure highly on the menu of such fish as the cod. The following streamer Jig is extremely easy to construct and its colour range can be a matter of personal choice of the angler. The head of the jig is made from the round ledger weight used in fresh water angling. This lead weight is painted white, with a black pupil eye. Fluorescent paint can be

Fig. 46   Squid or Cuttle Jig

used, for many of the creatures of the deep have a natural luminescence or phosphorescence. The hole in the weight is slightly reamed out to take the head of the hook. As for the hook a long shank single can be used or even a long shank treble. All white, black and white, yellow and red, etc., etc., can be used, and because the head of the lure is slipped on to the line and is detached from the rest of the lure, different coloured bodies and flies can be changed, quite quickly.

HEAD. Round ledger weight painted with black and white eye.

BODY. Undressed or white fluorescent chenille or any other colour.

WING. Six saddle hackles surrounding the hook shank dyed or all white.

The illustration of the lure gives the reader a good idea what it looks like in comparison to a small American type jig lure.

The following transatlantic patterns are included for comparison, they may well prove attractive to some of our species. The types and range of fur and feathered lures vary from realistic copies of natural baitfish to exotic flies bordering on the ridiculous.

The originator of the world renowned Muddler Minnow, Dan Gapen, sells a range of tandem streamers for use in fresh and salt water. All utilise silver mylar strips.

Fresh 'N' Salt Streamer (Gapen)
Rear hook undressed.

BACK. Red feathers.

BODY. White feathers.

CHEEK. Silver mylar strips.

Another group of American salt-water lures are what they term the 'Multi Wings'. This type of fly is usually tied on a normal size hook, but the wing extends well beyond the bend of the hook. If the flies are tied on nickel hooks there is no need for a body dressing, but bodies of tinsel or chenille can be used. All of the flies have exaggerated heads with large white eyes, black pupil.

Black and White Multiwing

HACKLE. Collar long fibred black cock.

WING. Two black saddle hackles, two white saddle hackles.

Pink Multiwing

HACKLE. Pink collar hackle.

WING. Four pink saddle hackles.

Red and White Multiwing
HACKLE.   Red collar.
WING.   Four white saddle hackles.

Yellow Multiwing
HACKLE.   Yellow collar.
WING.   Four yellow saddle hackles.

Red and Yellow Multiwing
HACKLE.   Red collar hackle.
WING.   Four yellow saddle hackles.

Grizzle and Yellow Multiwing
HACKLE.   Yellow collar.
WING.   Two grizzle, two yellow saddle hackles.

A single hook lure that has been used in the States for Sailfish and the like again uses mylar strip for its flash. Once more a simple streamer bringing results.

Sailfish Fly
HOOK.   5/0.
BODY.   Heavy white chenille.
WING.   Four long (6 in) saddle hackles white.
CHEEK.   Broad strips of mylar.

The Bonefish or Ladyfish is a highly sought after fish found in the warmer waters of the world. The Bahamas is one such area

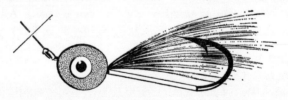

Fig. 47   An American Type Hair Jig.

famed for these sporting fish that freely take a fly. In past years they were sought after with salmon flies but a series of bucktails has been evolved expressly for bonefish. These flies may well be worth a try in our home waters for bass and the like.

Like the multiwing flies the Bonefish Bucktails utilise normal shank hooks. Goat hair, polar bear hair, or bucktail can be used for wings.

Brown and White Bonefish Bucktail

BODY. Brown chenille or wool.
HACKLE. White collar.
WING. Brown bucktail extending well beyond the hook.
HEAD. Red.

White Bonefish Bucktail

BODY. White chenille.
HACKLE. White collar.
WING. White bucktail.
HEAD. Red.

Yellow Bonefish Bucktail

BODY. Yellow chenille.
HACKLE. Yellow collar.
WING. Yellow bucktail.
HEAD. Red.

Yellow and White Bonefish Bucktail

BODY. White chenille.
HACKLE. White collar.
WING. Yellow bucktail.
HEAD. Red.

Combinations involving blues, green, blacks etc. can be used and as will be appreciated the number of such combinations is limitless.

Index